PRAISE FOR *In Search of the Divine Mother:*

"For readers struggling with complex issues of the master-disciple relationship, and the mind-bending clash of the skeptical mind with the mystic view, Goodman's superb book will come as a long-awaited reality check. Both analytical and profoundly personal, *In Search of the Divine Mother*—the only reliable biography to date of the modern master known as Mother Meera—is an illuminating account of the author's efforts to separate truth from make-believe and to bridge the gap between the inner and outer teacher. Gifted with the ironic eye of a novelist and the tender heart of a born seeker, Goodman manages to explode the legend surrounding Mother Meera while preserving the mystery behind her silent touch. Very inspiring."

—Mark Matousek, author of *Sex Death Enlightenment*

"A significant, illuminating contribution to the anatomy of the guru-disciple relationship."

—Olga Kharitidi, M.D., author of *Entering the Circle*

In Search of
THE DIVINE MOTHER

THE MYSTERY OF MOTHER MEERA
Encountering a Contemporary Mystic

Martin Goodman

HarperSanFrancisco
A Division of HarperCollins*Publishers*

HarperSanFrancisco and the author, in association with The Basic
Foundation, a not-for-profit organization whose primary mission
is reforestation, will facilitate the planting of two trees for every
one tree used in the manufacture of this book.

A TREE CLAUSE BOOK

HarperCollins Web Site: http://www.harpercollins.com
HarperCollins®, ♣ ®, HarperSanFrancisco™, and A TREE
CLAUSE BOOK are trademarks of HarperCollins Publishers Inc.

Book design by Martha Blegen

FIRST EDITION

Library of Congress Cataloging-in-Publication Data
Goodman, Martin.
In search of the divine mother : the mystery of Mother Meera :
encountering a contemporary mystic / Martin Goodman. —1st ed.
p.   cm.
ISBN 0–06–251509–8 (cloth)
ISBN 0–06–251510–1 (pbk.)
1. Meera, Mother.   2. Goodman, Martin.   3. Spiritual biography.
I. Title.
BL73.M44G66   1998
299'.93—dc21   97-38365

98 99 00 01 02 ❖ RRDH 10 9 8 7 6 5 4 3 2 1

For my mother,
Kathleen,
and my sisters,
Michelle and Elizabeth

Contents

Acknowledgments

Sometimes it feels as though this book was written against all the odds. In fact it flows from stories told by the families, friends, devotees, and acquaintances of Mother Meera in Europe, India, and America. Some are to be found by name within the pages of this book, and many others are there in spirit. I thank them for all their kindness, their memories, and their efforts.

My partner, James Thornton, has shared this journey throughout. The book stems from his suggestion, and there have been many times when he must have regretted its existence. As each fresh draft rolled out, he was there with his love and his editing skills to read through every page. He has been manful enough to set aside his own pattern of devotion, and his own feelings, in order to allow me the space to pursue my journey to the hilt. Much of the book's understanding of Aurobindo's philosophy comes through him, and the book has taken shape through countless hours, days, and months of discussion. The responsibility for the book is mine, but I am very happy for the extent to which it is also a product of our shared life.

Trevor O'Neill read an early draft of this book and dared to give an honest response. He helped the book shed its anger and helped me to honor the transformative effects of Mother Meera's presence in my life. I thank him for being there when I needed him.

Without John Loudon's commitment to this book, it would not have been written. I am honored to have his editorial experience and skills behind me, and I thank him for his daring and his judgment. I am grateful too for the impeccable and insightful support of Karen Levine, the book's assistant editor. The interest of my agent, Andrew Blauner, did not stop at placing the book; his care extended to a close and helpful reading of the final manuscript.

One of the greatest gifts of my visits to Thalheim is the number of special friends I made there. Their abiding friendship has helped fuel this book.

PART I

A Journey into Devotion

CHAPTER I

Meeting the Gaze

I am walking down the hill toward a German village because people say God lives there. She is at home for the evening and receiving visitors.

Two old men sit on a bench beside the path. They wear flat caps and gray cardigans and trousers, and their stomachs roll generously inside their white shirts. Their faces are gray too, but touched into color by the evening sunlight.

"Where are you going?" one asks.

I point across the fields. "Down to the village of Thalheim. To visit Mother Meera."

"Are you a Catholic?" The man on the right lifts his left hand a little. He is showing me a half-scale model of Jesus that stands behind him. Its flesh newly painted, the model is nailed to a large cross that stands in front of a broad, leaf-filled bush.

"No."

"Where are you from?"

"England."

"Then you must be Christian. Why do you come? Why do people come from all over the world? What do they expect from this Mother Meera?"

His companion looks up.

"She doesn't perform any miracles, you know," he advises.

"I know. I don't want miracles," I lie. We all would like some miracles, even if we don't believe in them. "I'm a writer. I have to see things for myself so I can write about them."

"Well then, that's different," they both agree, for these two ancient Germans are practical men.

Like Teutonic knights of old who guard the way, they let me pass.

⚯

THIS IS THE SUMMER OF 1991. Pears ripen on the trees beside the lanes, the forests and lands are green. The village of Thalheim nestles in a basin formed of wooded hills and fields. The spire of St. Stephen's church rises from the center of the village, and streets lined with solid, substantial houses radiate from it. A public bar, "The Hunter's Rest," sits below the church, and the village supports a small baker's, a grocer's, and a savings bank. People who live in Thalheim do not chase excitement. They opt for comfort, a family life lived within the expansive walls of home, and a barrier of miles of gentle countryside between themselves and the outside world.

Mother Meera lives in one of these houses. The stream that crosses her rear garden forms one of the boundaries of the village. The broad hill that rises beyond it is uncluttered by housing.

In 1991 the organization of these evenings with Mother Meera is still loose. People are mostly drawn by word of mouth. They do not need to make reservations, and all who come can be accommodated. Many fly into the international airport at Frankfurt. "Do people live here?" Mother Meera once asked in surprise as she was driven through that city. Her village is little more than an hour's drive away, but it lies in a different world.

That evening there are about sixty of us. We mill around the courtyard of the house, some trying words of contact with strangers, others maintaining silence. We are preparing to enter a holy and unfamiliar space. We slow our movements down and soften our noise.

The door of the house opens. A woman steps back in a rustle of thick silk to let us enter. The orange of her sari, rich with embroidery, suits her well. It shines like a beacon.

"Thank you," she says when I compliment her on the fact; she beams with pleasure that her appearance is noticed. "In India, orange is the color of sacrifice."

This is Adilakshmi. Her long black hair is drawn tightly back above her ears. Her face is round, her cheeks often plumped by smiles. Her manner at these public gatherings was practiced during her years as a teacher of young children in an Indian ashram. She is friendly, finds kind words to say, and directs people to appropriate seats. But she also picks out one person from among the crowd to whom she gives specific instructions—to move, to be quiet—thereby asserting her authority over the group.

Her manner is also the manner of a child, the child who is favored by the teacher and put in command of the class. Her eyes are bright. She is delighted to have this role to play and to be seen performing it well.

Although she is almost seventeen years older than Mother Meera, her childlike role is appropriate. Adilakshmi views Mother Meera as the Divine Mother. In the West we are familiar with a masculine version of God, as in God the Father. This God once became incarnate on earth through his son, Jesus Christ. The feminine version of God, the Divine Mother, some find in the Virgin Mary. The Divine Mother is worshiped in many forms throughout India, where she is considered responsible for the creative cycle of life. She is the force behind birth into life, growth through life, and transformation through death. She sometimes comes to earth in female form. For Adilakshmi, Mother Meera is unquestionably this rarest of beings, the supreme Divine Mother, a direct incarnation of God on earth.

◆

WE WALK IN OUR SOCKS across the gray marble floor of the audience room. It is large enough to seat us all comfortably, in rows of white plastic chairs. The chairs are grouped on either side of the center of the hall. The center is cleared for any visitors who prefer to sit on cushions on the floor, but mostly it gives people a clear passage up to the feet of Mother Meera. She will sit in an armchair set against the wall to face this vacant space.

The room settles into silence. The silence is individual at first, as people place themselves in this new environment. Then the individual silences become aware of each other, they touch, they merge, and a general silence grows to contain everybody and gather focus. It reaches out through the doorway and probes the unseen staircase that leads to Mother Meera's apartment two floors above. The church clock strikes seven but we already know the time, for this is the hour of Mother Meera's appearance, and expectation has peaked. We rise to our feet and listen for the first distant whisper of her approach.

The stage is set. A collective silence holds the audience. As the principal figure enters, we note her costume is superb. Mother Meera wears a sari of deep purple, alight with embroidery of silver thread.

Whereas Adilakshmi fills her sari amply and splendidly, Mother Meera barely has a body at all. She is short and slight. Thick socks cover her feet, which are hidden below the sari's silk. Her eyes look to the floor as she shuffles forward. This is not the entrance of a crowd pleaser. It is the entrance of someone who chooses to be lost in a crowd if she has to come out at all.

She seats herself in the armchair, and the audience sits too. For those of us used to more entertainment than this, the evening will seem long. There will be no amusement. There will be nothing to distract anyone from a very personal view of the evening's experience.

———◇———

ADILAKSHMI IS THE FIRST TO MOVE. She rises from her chair, and the thick silk of her sari crackles as she kneels on the carpet in front of Mother Meera's feet. She shuffles forward so her head is bowed between Mother Meera's knees. Adilakshmi's hands clasp the toes of the feet in front of her, and she closes her eyes. Mother Meera reaches forward. Her fingers press against the sides of Adilakshmi's head, a fingertip hold of gentle pressure.

We newcomers sit in the front rows to watch and learn from Adilakshmi's example.

How fast do we move? How close do we kneel? How low do we drop our heads? What do we do with our hands?

As Adilakshmi moves, we assemble our answers. We learn what to do with our bodies while the bigger questions remain.

What will happen to our spirit? What will stir in our soul?

———◇———

ADILAKSHMI HAS NO SUCH QUESTIONS in this time of being with Mother Meera. She knows that the transformative power of God flows through Mother Meera's hands. Such knowledge forms the mainstay of her life. She uses her energy to serve that knowledge, not to question it. Mother Meera's fingers move lightly across her scalp, movements marked by the slightest shifts and the gentlest pressures, as she adjusts lines of energy within Adilakshmi's body.

In her book *Answers,* Mother Meera speaks about two sets of lines. While Adilakshmi knows about their existence, she cannot experience them, for the lines can only be seen by such supreme beings as Mother Meera asserts herself to be.

One set of lines is white. These lines start at the toes, rise up the back of the legs, and connect into a single line at the base of the spine, which then continues up through the crown of the head.

The touch of Mother Meera's hands causes a white light to rise along these lines, somewhat like the line of mercury in a thermometer. Sometimes this light gets stuck at a certain height, sometimes it climbs higher, and just occasionally it sinks. The light shows the degree of a person's spiritual evolution. Should the light shoot up between Mother Meera's hands, bursting through the crown of the supplicant's head, then the person has evolved beyond the state of spiritual visions and glimpses of God. That being has reached a state of perpetual union with God.

Mother Meera's fingers work with barely detectable pressure. This is no machine shop for the soul, where hands plunge in to whisk from nowhere a state of enlightened bliss. One careless move, one casual slip of attention, and these lines of energy within a person's being might break and the person might die. The adjustments worked by Mother Meera's fingers can be compared to the care needed to straighten out a tight, tangled mass of cotton thread. Yanking at the thread will not work. Knot by knot the thread has to be untied, to be loosened from its bounds, in work of infinite patience. The knots in a person's white lines block the flow of spiritual energy. They are caused by things like doubt or personal injury.

The second set of lines, also visible only to divine beings, is red. These rise from the toes up the sides of the legs. When these red lines join at the base of the spine with the white line, the person is assured of permanent detachment from all desires other than the desire for the immanence of God.

In working with these lines, Mother Meera is working on the structure of the soul. She finds it hard to describe what the soul looks like, but sees it as a mixture of light and shadow. This light and shadow form a body, the soul's body, which rests inside the physical body.

Her hands rest on a person's head for around twenty seconds. As Mother Meera releases the fingertip hold on Adilakshmi's head, Adilakshmi sits back on her heels and opens her eyes. She is now staring into the eyes of Mother Meera, who gazes back at her.

This is all we newcomers see—two women bright in their Indian saris, one kneeling and one sitting, looking into the other's eyes. The younger woman's head pulses backward and forward slightly, but her eyes do not blink.

We know how hard it is for any two people to maintain full eye contact. There is a powerful charge that soon becomes too much to bear. One or the other soon has to look away or break into laughter. Here at the audiences with Mother Meera, laughter is not an appropriate option. The force that passes from Mother Meera's eyes has to be accepted and dealt with in some other way.

Adilakshmi opens her eyes not so much to see as to be seen.

There are two ways of seeing. One is what Sufis call "solar," when an active sight energy beams from our own eyes. Such a look projects power. The other way of seeing is "lunar," which is more passive, less focused. There is trust involved in such a look, for it means our defenses are down and we are allowing the other person in.

Adilakshmi opens her eyes in a lunar gaze. The look from Mother Meera's eyes enters her and scans for any areas of difficulty in her life. Along with the gaze from Mother Meera's eyes comes an infusion of light, light designed to heal wounds within the psyche and give a person sufficient power to move from the perspective of the personality to a divine perspective.

There is no challenge involved at this point. This is not one woman staring as the other stares back. Instead, one offers the gift of her soft, penetrative gaze, and the other offers the gift of acceptance. Adilakshmi removes the shields we often place before our

eyes and opens herself before the eyes of Mother Meera. In opening herself in this way, she is also opening the cells of her entire
being to the transformative power of divine light that now fills her.

Mother Meera closes her eyes and drops her head a little. Adilakshmi stands and returns to her seat. It is the next person's turn.

━━◇━━

MOST OF THE CHAIRS in the room are plastic. One chair stands out
among them, sturdier and made of pine. It is placed near Mother
Meera, slightly in front of her with a view of her in profile. It is
called "the waiting chair." When Adilakshmi kneels in front of
Mother Meera, someone moves to sit in this chair and begins
"waiting." That person is next to kneel before Mother Meera after
Adilakshmi rises.

There is no roster. There are no spoken commands, not even a
silent gesture. Silence envelopes the gathering for the entire dura-
tion of Mother Meera's presence in the room, and the only movement is the movement of individuals, one at a time, up to the
waiting chair.

There is no jostling, no competing, no obvious sign of impa-
tience. When the time comes for someone to approach the chair,
one person stands, and only one. From somewhere within the silence, people have perceived a sense of order. Some inner call
prompts them to stand—some intuition, some desperation perhaps, some moment of longing.

For us new visitors there is an element of stage fright too. The
smoothness of the operation highlights our own sense of awk-
wardness. We fear clumsiness or error. We fear the unknown too,
a fear that comes whenever we surrender the familiar practice of
our lives.

And it is also quite common for those who have not been to
one of these gatherings before to feel a pain. As I sit on the waiting chair for the very first time, my heart tries to escape. It pounds
against my chest. Each beat is measured to stop just this side of a
heart attack, beat after beat after beat.

A baby might feel a heartbeat like this when it is born—a sudden, shocking rush of life that seems like the edge of death.

The person before me rises. I dive to the floor and plant my hands on the ground on either side of Mother Meera's feet. The Hindu custom of clutching a master's feet seems indelicate and presumptuous to me with my Western ways.

My eyes are closed. I come to know Mother Meera through her touch. The lightness of her tiny fingers plays itself about my head. It is a hold, but not a grip. A shower of warm rain might exert a similar pressure.

Then the hands are lifted. I feel the loss of their weight, though the pressure of Mother Meera's fingertip hold still lingers and will return over the days to come.

Sitting back, I open my eyes. I keep my glasses on, for I want to see as much as I want to be seen. This young Indian woman I have never met opens her eyes before me.

It is a gesture of astonishing intimacy, the eyes wide and round, hazel brown merging into the black spots at their centers. Yet while the eyes are supposedly reading the condition of my life and suffusing me with light, they do not seem invasive. It is like looking into a broad expanse of water, as soft as that, a look that washes all around me.

Her face is without expression, but she is also young. Youth has an expression of its own that coats a young face even in repose. I look at Mother Meera, watch some wave pass above the skin of her cheeks to ease them into an invisible smile, and catch some gleam of play and love in her eyes.

Then the eyelashes, so long and so black, slowly close over her eyes. She tilts her head forward and it is time for me to stand.

As I walk back to my chair, her hands have already alighted on another person's head.

———◇———

THERE IS A STILLNESS AT THE END, after everyone who wishes to approach Mother Meera has done so. She sits, regarding her knees, in case anyone needs this extra time to come to her. Then she stands.

Everyone rises as she walks out of the room. Bodies stretch and language slowly returns. For more than two hours no one has spoken, no one has left the room. Some have been bored, some in bliss, but everybody has shared in a period of meditation. It is unusual to sit in silence for so long. Many are pleased with their own endurance, just as they are delighted to be free to move and talk again.

———◇———

I WALK WITH A YOUNG MAN back up the hill toward the lights of the village where we are staying. This is his first time too. He is dressed all in white, with the slightest flush of pink to his pale skin. His hair is dark and floats in waves from his head. He seems ethereal, as though he has yet to learn to walk on the earth and so floats just above it. I could not guess his nationality to look at him, but he is English drawn from a line of exiled Russian aristocracy.

"Isn't it wonderful?" he says. All his statements are shared as questions. "Aren't we lucky, so very lucky, to be devotees of the Divine Mother?"

The words waft toward me and his smile follows behind. The speech seems silly but sweet. I do not know what a divine mother is, let alone feel I have met one. The term "devotee" shocks me. I am too fond of my common sense to imagine I can ever be one of those. But the young man is well-intentioned and happy, so I smile back.

Mother Meera is in her apartment at the top of the house, making her usual cup of instant coffee, as I walk up the hill and away. I think I am leaving her behind. I don't yet understand the effect of gazing into her eyes. I don't know that something of Mother Meera now travels with me. I have just encountered what will grow to become the greatest mystery of my life.

Though I will come back to Thalheim and Mother Meera, part of me is already fixed in the landscape. It never leaves.

CHAPTER 2

Adventures in a German Village

The village of Dorndorf is raked along a hill-side near its heights. I come to know it well through several subsequent visits, staying for two weeks at a time. There is a tradition of guest houses here, catering to visitors who come to walk or hunt the forest trails. Now an astonishing range of foreigners sweeps in to fill all the rooms, and a bed-and-breakfast business expands through family homes. The village of Thalheim, half an hour's walk below, has no accommodation, so Dorndorf is favored ground for those who wish to visit Mother Meera without a car.

It is easy to spot these visitors around the landscape. Locals have a fixed reason for any walk they happen to be on. The purpose of their walk rests in their destination. Devotees are different. They drift like pollen or snowflakes, depending on the season. They are filling in time between Mother Meera's four public sessions each week, Friday through Monday evenings. Some sense of calm soaks from the countryside into their systems as they walk. They are happy. Their faces bloom with the passivity of the moon, eyes sparkle and smiles beam.

For some part of each day, they will very likely surprise themselves by returning to their rooms and surrendering to deep sleep. This German valley with its dark forests, soft hills, and gabled houses is something of a fairy-tale realm. Enter this land, and you feel the urge to slumber. For very many who come to see Mother Meera, one of the biggest surprises is an irresistible drowsiness. In their regular lives they might well be dynamic; now they simply long to fall asleep.

A book published by Mother Meera's own organization and called *The Mother* contains many early verbatim accounts of her meetings with God. One of them serves to offer some explanation for the waves of sleepiness experienced in Thalheim. Mother Meera asks God a question:

As spirituality grows, our mind and vital become weak. Why is this?

The word "vital" carries its own gloss in Indian spiritual circles. It bears the suggestion of emotional forces, unseen powers that emanate from a person's psyche, as distinct from the touch of the cosmic, divine force. People will often mistake what is "vital," unseen powers that stem from their life, for what is "spiritual."

God replies to Mother Meera's question:

The physical, vital, and mental abilities are changed into a greater power. Therefore these normal parts of the human being become weak, as they surrender their strength to that spiritual power.

This tiredness does not happen to everyone who comes, but it is typical. It is as though bodies recognize that the focus has shifted away from them toward the soul. They accept with grace and delight and swoon away from busyness into rest.

One common walking route around the valley leads people to the summit of Blasiussberg. Within the general heaving round-ness of the landscape, this particular hill stands out as higher and more pointed. A history of worship there stretches back through millennia, when particular sites in the region were held as sacred to gods like Wotan.

Now Roman Catholicism is the dominant force. A path up the hillside passes a series of shrines, bas-reliefs in iron marking the Stations of the Cross. The walk narrates Jesus' passage through crucifixion to resurrection. The summit levels out into an open-air altar and gathering ground. An inscription dedicates this space to those who gave their lives in the twentieth century's world wars. The church of St. Blasiuss stands at one edge of the hilltop. If we lift the latch on its oak door, we are free to step inside.

Wooden carvings of saints are mounted on the high white walls of its interior, while a hefty wooden Madonna cradles her infant to the side of the main altar. Many devotees of the Virgin Mary have fixed plaques to the walls beside her, thanking her for successful intercession in the problems of their lives, while candles usually glow before her.

Many of those who come to see Mother Meera feel themselves a part of the Christian tradition. Others are happy to view the Virgin Mary as an earlier incarnation of the Divine Mother. And a story passes around that Blasiussberg is a sacred hill and that Mother Meera has based herself nearby so it can help her anchor the light she brings to the earth.

On the opposite side of the altar to the Madonna sits an ancient rock grooved into the shape of a seat. The story continues that this stone has unique powers of its own, that much of Mother Meera's work is focused through it.

When I later ask Mother Meera whether Blasiussberg is espe-cially sacred, her reply is that it is not especially so to her. She of-fers a range of other replies to similar questions, most of them dismissive. She gains no support in her work from any particular place. Similarly, though some devotees associate her with the peacock, she has no special relationship with any bird or animal. Questions about what light she is working with are deemed silly, because all light is her light. She has no favorite songs, no favorite people, no special attachment to any place; gods and goddesses don't appear to her in any human form; she expects nothing of anyone; and she is in good health, despite constant rumors to the contrary.

Such stories continue to trickle through the devotees' grapevine, however, in spite of denials. They are part of the process of devotion.

——◇——

EARLY FEARS AMONG THE LOCALS, when an influx of foreign devotees to these German villages bore the air of an alien invasion, soon eased. The foreigners are personable people on the whole, representatives of professional classes rather than hippiedom. They do not close themselves into an ashram and away from the regular world. They do not gather their resources to buy up homes in the neighborhood and threaten the traditional community. They come, live quietly for a short while, then move away again. The local economy prospers and all seems fine.

Old folk stop me in the streets or on the paths. They have stories from the Second World War that they have been keeping inside them for decades. Now foreigners have entered their village. The residents' isolation is broken. Their conversations become monologues, catalogues of the personal tragedies of war, as tears gather in their eyes and glisten on their cheeks.

——◇——

DOWN BELOW IN THE VILLAGE of Thalheim an old man comes out to sweep a thin fall of snow from the sidewalk in front of his house. In the summer he takes a broom to the dust that edges the street, collects it in a dustpan, wraps it up in a plastic bag, and takes it indoors. The houses put up an orderly front, and their walls contain great privacy.

It is a good place for a young Indian woman to come and set up her home as God on earth. The standard house size in the village is enormous, and as long as you keep to yourself and don't bother the neighbors, you will be left to your own devices.

Nature knows its place in the region too. In some areas notices advise that wildlife is protected. In others, it is shot. Wooden keeps are raised on high stilts so hunters can stay hidden while their prey draws close. The landscape is folded into hills rather than mountains. Deer leap across the bracken when disturbed, wild boar go charging through it, and buzzards shoot out in flight from treetops. Forests are expansive but not dense. They grow to be harvested, and an extensive network of footpaths is maintained both through and between them.

The highest edge of the village is bordered by the acres of St. Stephen's churchyard, which itself expires into the countryside. This churchyard contains a grave that is important to Mother Meera. For that reason, it has also become a pilgrimage site for devotees.

Most know little of the man who was buried here in 1985. Their main contact with him comes from the room in which they sit for their audience with Mother Meera, for his portrait is prominent on a wall. The man turns within the frame to smile out at onlookers, his round head crowned with the crisp white lines of an Indian cotton cap, the canvas behind him painted a rich dark green.

Devotees are likely to know just a few stories about him. He is known as Mr. Reddy, sometimes called Mother Meera's uncle, who was responsible for bringing her from an Indian village to her position as a renowned spiritual figure in the West. Those who think in terms of Mother Meera's special divinity are led to understand that she cannot be thought of as separate from Mr. Reddy. The two of them are twinned in a divine mission to earth. While his body rests in this grave, the teaching tells that his presence around Mother Meera is as strong as it was in life.

The headstone and the slab of his grave are of a grained white marble imported from Portugal. A cast-iron lantern that stands

upon it is wrought in the shape of the Sanskrit word *Om*, the holy
symbol of all creation, and fashioned in the letters of Mr. Reddy's
native Telugu script.

A visit to this grave is part of my regular route of walks around
the villages. I look for some spiritual charge from the site, some
insight and understanding.

The process of walking helps me in another way too. One of
the attractions of Mother Meera is that she demands so little. She
asks for no money from me, demands no allegiance; whether I
come to see her or not is entirely up to me. Far from calling me to
leave my work, my family, or my religion, in her published words
she asks me to try to be with them more completely. The clearest
advice she gives, the only requirement for those who wish to follow her "way," is the constant repetition of a holy name.

This does not have to be her name. Any holy name that
resounds for the individual will do. For myself, I know no other
holy name more surely than hers. There is none that calls me
especially. In coming to see her I am on a pilgrimage, and the
pilgrimage is an experiment. Part of my experiment involves living by the rules.

I not only choose her name to repeat. To complete the business
I adopt her entire mantra. *Om Namo Bhagavate Mata Meera.* It
means little to me but I learn the sounds. I seek to make a silent
repetition of this mantra a constant in my life, a thrum of sound
that backs all waking and sleeping hours. It is hard. My mind
wanders away from it. These walks around the countryside are my
method of drilling in the practice. My footfalls are reminders that
the mantra is lost, and when I realize this I resume it again.

Om Namo Bhagavate Mata Meera. I learn something of the
meaning of this Sanskrit phrase without its meaning very much.
Om is the sound of creation, holding all other sounds within itself. *Namo* has the sense of being drawn into adoration and so
bowing down. *Bhagavate* suggests the most revered, the most
powerful of divine beings. *Mata* is "mother." The complete

mantra accompanies my steps down the hillside to the evening sessions in her silent company and then sounds with my tread back up the hill to my room and her photograph.

———◇———

THE PHOTOGRAPH IS AN EARLY ONE in black and white in which her hair is loose and frizzes with static electricity. A small store in Mother Meera's house does a whirl of business in such items in the minutes after her public sessions.

It is a Wednesday night—two days since my last encounter with Mother Meera and two days before my next. I am in my room writing a novel. I feel called to put down my pen and stare into the photo, which stands on the table beside me.

I bring it down to my lap and look into it, repeating Mother Meera's mantra to myself. An energy builds up inside me. It vibrates through my head. The room beyond the picture grows darker. The lightbulbs dim. Their energy is being drained out of them, drained out of the lightbulbs and into the picture.

The picture glows. Light haloes the edges of the young woman's head and shoulders first of all, a pure white light. It then traces patterns across her face. These patterns lead me into a period of deep meditation on two primal images from my own culture.

One is the picture of Christ's crucifixion, the head of Jesus drooping on the cross. For some time I see the image clearly, formed from light that passes up the bridge of Mother Meera's nose toward the devotional red kumkum spot on her forehead.

It is not my job simply to see it, to reflect upon it. It is for me to witness this sight as fully and completely as possible. I am looking at a man of supreme and perfect goodness, who came to earth and was treated in this grotesque and barbaric fashion. He was crucified because his goodness was a threat. The image of the crucified body is lost when it becomes a familiar symbol, just as Jesus is lost when we look up at him and address him simply as a friend. The crucifixion should affect us in two ways.

It can astonish us with its beauty, the supreme example of a man's total abandonment of his own self-interest. It is a shining expression of love.

It also calls us to responsibility. We must not see the crucifixion and simply pass by. Humanity was so repelled by the goodness of Jesus, so in terror of his example, that it hanged him to die and jeered as it watched. The crucifixion is our proof of our own human capacity to reject goodness. We must remember this, accept this possibility within ourselves, take care to look out into our world and see where the world acts in a similar mode of grievous wrong. We must look for this and then not simply stand by, not simply nod in recognition. We must witness the wrong in our bodies, see it as a wound to our humanity, and dare to stand and give full expression to our revulsion.

The image of the crucifixion is a call to action, a call to caring for a better world, a demand to follow Jesus Christ's example. We cannot act as though our own interests are different from the interests of all we see around us. There is only one way of acting for our own good—acting for the good of the world.

The second image of light that spins out from my small photograph of Mother Meera, the second image from my culture, is even more obviously a call to action in the world. Curiously, I come to see that the direction it gives me is different from the one I expect.

The picture of light is a distinct and shining figure of a chalice. This is the Holy Grail, the secret at the heart of Camelot. The quest for the Holy Grail leads out of our lives and into legend, away from the present and back through the past. The knights of King Arthur's court adventure through forests and realms of great daring, their search for a golden chalice also a search for the meaning of life.

As I meditate on this image now patterned by the light from Mother Meera's picture, I look into the symbol's source. I see that these forests of darkness are truly within ourselves, that the demons and dangers we meet there are the shadows and shames of our life. We have made the quest for the Holy Grail into a story and in so doing we have externalized it, but truly the journey we have to make is deep into our own being. The Holy Grail is not something that stands outside of ourselves. That is why it is so elusive, why it seems so very well hidden.

The Holy Grail is part of the human condition.

In my picture golden light moves up the side of the nose and across the brow, then arches up around the temples to form the outline of a golden chalice. Yet while the outline at its simplest may be the nose and brows, what it cups is our innate spiritual nature. Spiritual traditions locate the focus of this nature in the third eye, the spot in the forehead between the two visual eyes through which the harmony and oneness of creation is witnessed. This marks a way of looking out on the world, but from a position of internal balance. If we are calling for attention to be paid to ourselves, if we are obsessed with the drama of our individual lives, we will never look out on the world with sufficient clarity. We have to subdue the clamor in our own lives, heal the divisions spawned by our insecurity, before the chalice can be ours.

I meditate on the images of the crucifixion and the Grail, and two lessons are placed as seeds in my life. I must bear witness to the world and bring this witnessing back as a clear form of expression. And before I do so, before I have a right to say or write anything on what I find in the world outside, I must go on an intense journey into my own human condition. I must confront all that I do not like about myself before I can see the rest of life with any clarity.

The twin lessons are planted within me. The photo changes. The face stretches and contracts, begins to shift itself, as can happen to the appearance of a face as a rubber mask is being removed. And then it switches.

Flash. I am looking at Mother Meera's photo, but seeing someone else.

Flash. It changes again. And again. Every few seconds a different face appears. Sometimes it is a man, sometimes a woman, and sometimes the smiling face of Mother Meera interspersed between them. It is a shifting gallery of hundreds of portraits of humanity, face after face budding and blossoming through the outlines of the head in my little picture.

The show continues for hours. Whenever the process fades, I speak Mother Meera's mantra aloud instead of silently, and the increased energy gives a fresh charge to the photo.

This is a third lesson. I can look hard into the face of Mother Meera, but that face is not important. The purpose of my growing devotion is not worship of her. She is there, her face reappears as part of the gallery of portraits, but it gives way to the faces of others. My journey into the mystery of Mother Meera is a journey into the widest reaches of humanity. It is a journey into the essence of life.

In the early hours of the morning, I set the flashing photo to one side and leave it to fade back into its existence as a regular black and white snapshot. I don't need to hold on to this minor miracle, for I have its lessons inside me.

I lie on my bed and let myself rest in sleep.

———◇———

THERE IS AN ODDLY DISTURBING FACT about the children in these German villages, many of them blond and all of them fair-skinned: they are trained to say hello to strangers. As I walk along the sidewalks, the children greet me, then keep on walking. I am partly charmed and partly touched by guilt, feeling ashamed of my English society in which children are not so free. I know that young children are not to be approached, so I have blinkered myself into blindness. I have no natural response to such innocence.

I walk toward the railway station in a nearby village. A group of youngsters walk toward me. At the back of the group, near to the others but on his own, is a young man. I spot his youth, his beauty, his gentleness, the flop of his dark hair over his brow. And I look away.

This is the training of my lifetime. I follow the strictures of society rather than the truth of my own experience. I have learned that the gay part of my sexuality is bad, and so I act out of shame of it. This is a natural part of my being, and yet I label it sinful.

I hold my head up straight, restraining even my sidelong glances, as I walk past the young people.

"Hello," the young man says and shines a smile at me before walking on. It helps so much. I step beyond my guilt and walk more freely.

Miracles are often such little things in life.

＝◇＝

I WAKE ONE MORNING in my bedroom at a Dorndorf guest house with an idea in my head.

"Buy some flowers," the idea says. "Then walk down to Thalheim and give them to your friend James."

I have never bought flowers for another man. However, I am learning to accept these promptings that come into my head. They lead me beyond my code of behavior, which reflects my concern about how the world sees me. Instead, they show me a world that is fresher and more loving than I have ever dared to enjoy.

An Israeli woman approaches me at breakfast. "Are you walking down to Thalheim?" she asks.

The decision to do so fresh in my mind, I answer that I am.

"Then please can I walk with you? I'd like you to show me Mr. Reddy's grave. I've looked but I can't find it."

We leave the dining room, head off to the village florist, fill my backpack with a bunch of pink roses, and set off down the hill.

＝◇＝

WE TALK AS WE WALK the path down into the valley. The woman from Israel is visiting Mother Meera for the first time, and she tells me she is afraid. She knows friends who feel their lives have been in Mother Meera's hands for some time now. All these friends have experienced black times when they have been faced with onslaughts from their "demons." She does not want such a savage time for herself.

"They're not demons," I tell her. "Not in the satanic sense, the sense of evil forces set against you. Demons are simply aspects of ourselves we are not able to accept. My own demons have a lot to do with my sexuality, but there are many other types. Lack of conventional beauty, relative poverty, body odor, childhood abuse, failure to rise through the ranks at work. Everybody knows what they are ashamed of. That shame is their demon.

"We stuff this shame into the darkest recesses of ourselves, so no one will guess it's there. That's our terror. We fear that someone will guess at this aspect of ourselves and hate us for it. This shame forms our biggest fear, our biggest secret, our biggest lie— the lie that at heart we are basically unlovable. If anybody either guesses at our secret shame or reflects it back to us, we will fight them tooth and claw. We'll damn them to hell. Nobody must ever know this shameful fact about ourselves.

"We put so much energy into repressing this aspect of our being, focus so much intent on keeping it pressed away in the dark, that of course it becomes very powerful. It has much of our energy packed inside it. It becomes so strong it has to rise, has to burst out of the dark and into the light.

"That's what this way is. That's how I perceive the path with Mother Meera. It begins with discovering all that we hate about ourselves and bringing it up into the light. Once it's there, we look at it and find that it is blessed.

"That may sound heavy, but it's not. It's a way of letting heaviness go. Just think, you're walking along and suddenly your spirits sag. Something you see or something you hear upsets you. It stirs up some old pain of yours and churns you up inside. So what you do is notice this pain and let it go. You feel it rush up through the crown of your head and away. And you feel some blessing come back in return. You suddenly find yourself lighter and happier than you were before."

The woman is silent as we walk along a lane lined with pear trees. We pick up some ripe fruit that has fallen to the ground. Then she skips as she breaks out of her silence.

"I've got it," she says. "I know what my demon is. I know what there is in my life I've got to face up to."

She bites into the pear so that its juice explodes into her mouth.

"It's exciting, isn't it?" she says.

Juice trickles down from her lips as she smiles, trying to hold back a laugh until she has swallowed the fruit down.

—◇—

WE PASS THROUGH A FARMYARD on an unfamiliar route up to the grave. Tombstones in black, gray, and white are ranged along the slopes. The order and neatness of the paths in between them disguise the fact that I have lost my way. A hedge borders the road at the top of the slope. I let it lead me back to Mr. Reddy's grave.

We are almost there, my mission as guide accomplished, when a gate in the hedge opens. A woman walks through it. A light blue anorak quilted against the cold pads out her figure, but she is still tiny. It is Mother Meera.

Behind her walks Herbert, her husband. Thin of hair and stocky, he has a figure with the girth and sense of compressed energy that German chancellor Helmut Kohl, a politician much admired by Mother Meera, is seeking to make fashionable. Herbert wears an anorak too and is squeezed into a pair of jeans. He usually appears in public in more formal clothing, a combination of jacket, shirt, and tie in colors that clash in a bracing way. He stands as a sentinel at the front door on the evenings of public audiences, studying people through his glasses as they approach. He is expressionless and partially blocks the door so that people have to walk around him to get inside.

Mother Meera and Herbert have also come to visit Mr. Reddy's grave. We stay back as they step up to the marble slab and stand before it for a few minutes. As they leave, they turn to us. Mother Meera smiles.

As a child I once pulled an outer petal from a rosebud, and the bud instantly unfurled into an open flower of extravagant beauty. That was the first time I witnessed a transformation. This is the second.

I have never seen Mother Meera smile before. It is a wide smile with shining white teeth, an open-eyed smile that reflects the daylight, a smile that brings her whole face to life. It is such a marked change in a face I have grown intimate with over fourteen months, a face that has guided me from a photo when not there in real life, that its smile appears like the very invention of a smile. We work to elicit a smile from those we love, but I have done nothing for this smile. It comes as a gift. It renders my whole world less stern and more beautiful.

I know I am smiling in response, as is the Israeli woman beside me, for I see our smiles reflected in a smile that lights up Herbert's face. He is normally a dour man, but his eyes now sparkle and his face is recomposed in a roundness of joy.

The couple step out through the gate and along the road.

—◇—

THE ROSES BRING A SMILE from James too. It is a shy smile, a smile that shifts between other emotions, as he wonders what this gift of flowers might mean. He takes them to his room, where they will perfume the last week of his fourteen-month stay. He is about to leave this intense and prolonged meditation retreat and return to America. He comes back to usher the woman and me through a gabled barn to Mother Meera's garden and a meal of rice in the shade of an apple tree.

The Israeli woman's encounter with Mother Meera bubbles out as laughter, and James laughs in response. The garden fills with the sounds of shared laughter.

It will be almost two years before I see James again, as our lives work their way toward each other.

—◈—

BACK IN THE CITY OF GLASGOW, my home during these years, I drive out to see a friend in the countryside. It is a short and simple route along modest roads, a route I know well. Now I find I cannot manage it at all. I get locked on a six-lane highway I don't know how to exit. I keep circling around a traffic circle, not knowing why I am on it or where to leave it. I pull up and stare at stoplights that are green as cars blow their horns behind me. When I find myself driving across the frozen ruts of a plowed field, I recognize it is time to head home and take stock of my situation.

My visits to Mother Meera have had an effect I have not been prepared for. A great rush of energy was absorbed in each encounter with her. I walked from her public sessions and the German countryside reassured me. It extended my minutes with her through every moment of each week of my stay. That German village life was so clearly removed from my everyday working world that it provided no known context in which to examine myself.

Now that I have returned to that regular world, no great change is immediately apparent. This is for two reasons.

One is that the change is not complete, but ongoing. Life is changing, but the process of change is unfamiliar. I don't know what my life is changing into and cannot judge the stages as they happen. Every stage along the way is new. If I find a recipe for a cake, locate all the ingredients, but have never heard of or seen or tasted a cake before, I cannot judge it well from the beaten mess I put into the oven. I can take this mixture out every few minutes, wait for it to cool, and taste what is warm goo, but unless I wait I will never taste cake.

I am something like that cake. I am being cooked, being changed from inside. I can't know how I will taste and can't anticipate that moment of knowing. It is simply a matter of staying with the process long enough.

The other reason that this change stays hidden at first is that the change largely exists in my relationship with the world around me. I interact with the world more intensely than I did, look for perspectives that are not my own, shield myself less. It is only when I am back in my old pattern of relationships that I recognize my reactions no longer apply. I have a different way of seeing.

In the old way, everything was familiar and nothing could stay new for long. I saw everything in relation to everything else. If something novel came to my attention, I would find the aspects in it that reminded me of something else and make it belong within my view of the world as quickly as possible.

For example, a road that leads off my regular route I used to know only as the road I did not go down. An unfamiliar person passed on the street would simply be classed as a stranger. In the new way of seeing, the road that leads away from my destination bursts with possibilities for adventure. I see a total stranger and feel the rush of joy that comes from meeting a friend or perhaps a huge sadness at the apparent unhappiness in that person's life. Garbage on the street shines in plastic beauty, is radiant with snatches of color.

The focus of my new mode of perception is wider and much more open. While I am seeing more, taking in so much more from my environment than I previously did, I have not practiced the art of transforming everything I now receive. I have not learned to balance this new way of seeing with my old way of dealing with the world.

As with every new skill when we are starting out, we need to allow ourselves time. With a new language, we begin with some simple phrases. A new piece of music we play more slowly than one we are ready to perform in concert. In this instance I have to practice control over my new sense of awareness. I need time to admire a green traffic light for a beauty I have never seen before. In time I can balance this beauty with my knowledge of the code, and so drive at the sight of a green light rather than stop.

I stage my reentry more carefully after future visits to Germany. For a time I leave my car parked and become a pedestrian. I walk rather than drive, seek solitude as much as company, and honor the sounds I discover in what I used to think was silence.

Horses are blinkered so they can run without distractions. Now my blinkers are off. I love the distraction of every atom of beauty. It is a new state of being that is so much finer than the old. I shall learn to control it, but choose to enjoy it first of all. Lessons in life are often tough, but there is joy along the way. I set out to learn how to handle a perpetual sense of wonder.

CHAPTER 3

The Background to a Quest

The elderly Germans rise early for breakfast. They sit at tables by the windows, silhouettes in front of the bright screen of daylight. They have been coming to this guest house for many years, living life gently for a few vacation days and enjoying the forest. They murmur among themselves as they eat their bread and cheese and nod their heads politely as they stand to leave the dining room.

"Thank God they've gone," a bearded American in the center of the room announces. "They were so loud. And I couldn't understand a word they said."

He and his colleagues continue their conversation. The dining room is an echo chamber that has been reverberating with their talk for an hour already. They are performers, used to addressing large audiences and being the focus of attention. They are healers, they are visionaries, they give courses in metaphysics in universities in Australia and America. They are delighted to have discovered each other in this German hideaway.

They compare their dreams, their visions, and their spiritual awakenings. They compete to see who has the most forthright interpretation of aspects of the philosophy of the Indian sage Sri Aurobindo. They condemn with theatrical gestures the theatricality they find in *Hidden Journey,* the book by Andrew Harvey that has led them all to come and visit Mother Meera.

Others on a similar pilgrimage sit singly or in pairs. The volume and tone of this central disquisition does not allow them to have conversations or thoughts of their own. As the coffeepots are refilled, they leave their own tables and edge nearer.

Those in the central group shift marginally sideways on their bench seats as a mark of welcome. It is the welcome of satisfied cats. They angle their heads to receive the strokes of the newcomers' attention, but do nothing to find out who these newcomers are. They know them as spectators who have brought along their admiration, and that is enough.

Those in the central group dab their talking mouths with their napkins, then rise to leave the room.

=◇=

I HAVE BEEN MAKING my visits to Germany for some time. I am able to sit at my corner table and observe the morning's show without being attracted to it. I reflect on my own experience and see this show as an aspect of Mother Meera's work at play.

Mother Meera herself stays silent in her public role. Few who come to see her will ever hear her speak. Two books draw on her responses to questions during her years in the West. *Answers* (1991) contains material from a rare public question-and-answer session in New York, as well as questions relayed to Mother Meera over the phone during the weekly hours she is available for such questioning. *Answers Part 2* (1997) has its source in similar telephone questions, as well as questions invited from favored devotees.

But even with the availability of this printed material, many devotees feel the need of human contact, the need to share their experiences and questions with other devotees, and have a way of gravitating toward one another to form smaller or larger groups. I use the term "constellation" to describe this phenomenon. There is some delicate touch that guides one person to meet another. Like drops of water on a windowpane, they resist each other for a moment. They stay closed in their own skin, their own particular formation. Then the skins melt. The two drops rush into each other and then continue their passage within the stream.

I meet one woman on a bus during my first moments in Thalheim. We don't speak. We simply notice each other. Our first conversation follows my first evening with Mother Meera. We sit at a table and discover we are both novelists, represented by the same literary agency. We begin our journey into a very dear and vital, and we hope everlasting, friendship.

It is on this visit that I meet James, the man who is to become my life partner. He is a shadow in a corner of the dining room, a face that seldom peers above the covers of a vast blue tome of Tibetan doctrine and, when it does, looks down again at once. I embark on a game of easing him from the grip of his considerable intellect and back into play. He works on helping me articulate things I have never allowed myself to say and so encounter truth in a clearer way.

We go for walks in the countryside. Sometimes as we walk a sentence forms in my head. It is a sentence from my secret history, a fact from my life that I have never spoken because it shames me. As the sentence comes into my head, all other speech vanishes. It seems that I have to tell my story to this man or never speak again. I laugh, tell James my secret, and find that he accepts it without judgment. My shame about my own story is released. Our conversation flows.

Opportunities are always there to loosen ourselves from our own inhibitions, to act from our natural state rather than some stifling sense of decorum. Ever since I first looked into the eyes of Mother Meera, I have found I have the courage to accept these opportunities as they arise. I tune in to more subtle promptings and follow their lead.

Speaking unspoken words to someone who will listen is one example of this. My relationship with James is helped by another example. As we close a visit to the nearby city of Limburg, we look around its cathedral. We stand near the baptismal font, listening to the organ thundering its music around the vaulted ceilings, and a message lodges itself in my mind.

"Hug this man," it says.

The message is accompanied by a column of energy that drops into my head. Both the message and the energy surprise me.

"I'm sorry," is my response. "I don't hug men. And I certainly don't do so in a cathedral. That is wildly inappropriate."

The message persists. The column of energy courses through me. I look at James, who is blinking at the wonders of the music and the beauty of the cathedral, and see how dear and fragile he looks. I flap my arms very briefly around him, then let go.

This is the beginning of guidance that will help me through the early stages of our relationship. My self-hatred keeps coming back. I begin to withdraw from moments of intimacy and retreat into a definition of myself.

"I'm not like this," I say. "This is not what I do."

At these points this column of love pours into my head. It wipes me clean of such thoughts. This flood of love that fills me asks to be honored. I learn to express it rather than to resist it, to give love in a situation in which withdrawing it would only amplify the other person's pain. I learn to set aside my self-defense and see that someone else's needs deserve greater respect than my own fears for myself.

And in meeting someone else's needs in such a way, my own needs are met.

There is a certain daring in letting ourselves be loved. I start to dare after looking into Mother Meera's eyes. The eyes seem to offer love rather than judgment. Their look starts the process in me that sees me release my shame.

As yet I know nothing of regrettable remarks Mother Meera will make on the issue of homosexuality. For now it is enough that I embark on a journey that challenges my own homophobia, that helps me confront my shame at my own homosexuality.

In time I will come to find my sexuality blessed rather than damned. It is an energy, a force, like any other. Homosexual or heterosexual, sexuality needs to be expressed, for there is nothing natural about an energy that is repressed. Energy must flow. A sexual partner is a blessing, but the energy of sex can flow without the act. If repressed, sexuality bursts out as acts of anger or meanness.

If accepted, sexuality flows as one more good and vital force in a person's life.

James remains in the small German village for fourteen months after our first visit, a spiritual hermit facing all the shadows of his life. He and I share more walks and time on each of my visits, but thoughts of a relationship are never entertained. Neither of us is the other's type. He leaves to return to America. On a subsequent visit to Mother Meera's house, he dares to pose a request that is as frank about his needs as he knows how to express them. Remembering Mother Meera's advice that we find the courage to ask for anything in life, he sits down and writes on a piece of paper what he most wants.

"Mother, will you help me find a man to be my lover and life companion?"

Adilakshmi carries the question away, then hurries back with the response.

"Mother says yes!"

Adilakshmi joins him in sitting down and breaking through giggles into laughter, a mixture of joy and relief.

The following day he boards a plane to come and visit me on the English coast. The two drops of our existence merge and rush along in the stream.

———◇———

I WATCH THE VOCAL METAPHYSICIANS at the breakfast table and the others who shifted tentatively around in search of each other. Constellations are forming. Each person finds a match, the one best suited to share the journey that is to come.

These constellations are not restrictive. My constellation includes the woman and man who initially formed mine, yet they each in turn also belong to other constellations. Constellations merge and the patterns of friendship expand.

The phenomenon does not simply happen among those who visit Germany. I know of examples in an English village and a Japanese office, when people who were beginning their journey with Mother Meera's photograph as their starting point were brought into wholly unexpected contact with others also on the journey.

For many, these constellations of friendship are an essential part of the "silent way" of Mother Meera. They provide a network of support in the run of daily life that helps people dare to speak from their new awareness of life to people who are undergoing a similar process. In becoming devotees people become vulnerable to mystical openings, but the miracle of friendship is one of the truest miracles they will know.

———◇———

SOME TWENTY YEARS EARLIER I started the practice of Transcendental Meditation (TM). I traveled through Asia visiting holy sites. I read my way into the system of Gurdjieff and tried to adopt the

Baha'i faith. I spent time at the Findhorn Foundation in northern Scotland, and in the works of their associate David Spangler I found an intelligent commentary on the New Age. His books took the glimmerings of my perceptions and expanded them into a coherent philosophy that had the substance of a science.

Yet these are all behind me. They are completed stages in a journey that now continues beyond their reach. They are systems, and I want a way that is no system. They are communities, and in embracing those who can join them communities exclude those who cannot. I want a way that has all of life as its current and its pulse. The existence of these other spiritual paths is often predicated on a sense of wound. I want a way with a promise of wholeness. I will be a filament of life but an affiliate of no one.

Mother Meera moves and works through silence. She claims nothing, proclaims nothing, asks nothing, demands nothing. She works in seclusion in her apartment. There are no urgent missives to the world, no stream of directives channeled from God. She states her job as bringing a new light to all creation. I see her as someone who gathers and disseminates power, a power that generates growth in awareness and the force of creation. Even when she is seen as a distant speck walking through the German countryside, a bolt of energy can charge from her figure and hit the onlooker with the force of a moving truck. The sight of her smile can suffuse the body, atoms of being purring against each other and drifting dizzily through immediate space. But in her public appearances she is self-effacing almost to the point of extinction. There are only the unseen touch of her fingers and the look that is shared with her eyes.

In this act of vanishing, Mother Meera grows broader. Personality is removed so there is nothing to stick to, nothing to cling to. She does not want to attract you to herself, so you simply pass through her. This passing has the resonance of a hint of antimatter passing through a black hole and exploding into a cosmos. The other spiritual paths I have tried seemed to cramp life's potential in some way. Mother Meera seems broad enough to allow free flow to the full force of life.

————◇————

I TURN TO BOOKS to broaden the field of my experience. I had viewed Hinduism as some colorful but pagan religion. As I look more closely, I discover it is not a religion at all. Hinduism is an umbrella title sheltering a mass of belief systems. These spring from an Indian civilization that encourages a personalization of divine intuitions. When people are encouraged to see the divine in human form, they do so.

The divine has many aspects and some of these aspects appear as supreme within the scriptures of India. However, even these, such as the supreme god Shiva and his female counterpart Parvati, appear in many variants. They splinter into different aspects of themselves and, taking different names and different forms, are worshiped in various ways throughout India. Sometimes they have temples served by a hierarchy of priests and servants, but the principal genesis of all these branches of religion lies in individual human experience.

God forms no religions. They are formed from human perceptions of God.

I discover accounts of people who found so strong and personal a relationship with God that religions formed around them. Christopher Isherwood wrote an account of Ramakrishna, the nineteenth-century saint from Calcutta whose life was flooded with a constant awareness of the presence of the Divine Mother. I read Arthur Osborne's story of the life of Ramana Maharshi, who passed through an experience of death as a boy in southern India into an experience of total union with God as embodied in the sacred mountain Arunachala. I read Yogananda's exuberant tale of his travels through India and trust in God, *The Autobiography of a Yogi*.

I had previously studied Hinduism through the academic perspective of the West. These books bypass that critical, mental mode and allow me to look out from the heart of individual experience. From the examples of these holy men I learn that spiritual experience does not have to be channeled through religious institutions. It is open to direct, individual perception.

My reading widens. From the Indian scriptures and stories of saints I move my attention back to Christianity. Books on the early days of the church are interspersed with my reading of the New Testament. I am on an archaeological dig through the layers institutions have encrusted over the direct experience of Christ. When Christianity is peeled away, I catch something of the power of Jesus for the first time. I see a man who was born in Judaism, trained in Judaism, yet told that God did not need the filters of any church. Jesus is an example of the descent of God to earth. His was a body that opened to the full possibility of God and so was transfused with the magnitude of God in return.

I see this because I have been with Mother Meera. Holy people of old are brought alive for me through my acquaintance with her living example. I am learning to understand Mother Meera as an embodiment of God on earth.

As she sits in silent splendor, Mother Meera is detached from her own history. You go to her for her divinity, and that is what you get. Questions may arise. Why do I kneel in front of this young Indian woman? Where has she come from? What is she like when she is not being silent? What is it like to live as God? Why does she bother?

It is possible to set aside all such questions for a while, but they persist. They persist because they have answers that we can go on to find.

PART 2

The Life Story

CHAPTER 4

The Child Is Born

The horizon of the village of Chandepalle, in the southern Indian state of Andhra Pradesh, is a forest. Craftsmen carve flowers into its fallen timber. Painted sky blue, these streak as roof beams across the ceilings of the grander houses. Fields spread where wells can water them, bordered by ridges dug up from the land. Sometimes the earth turns to water, till young rice plants pierce the reflective surface and the water sinks back into mud.

A tracery of lanes links this village to others, narrow ways that channel through the countryside. In the seasons of monsoon the earth turns liquid and pulls at the feet and wheels of all that pass. The history of these journeys is baked into the ground for the hot months, when deep ruts gouged in the quagmire turn as solid as stone.

The lanes ferry produce to the markets and landowners to the banks. There is little need for most of the villagers to pass along them. Their kinship is with the land.

A wall divides two houses in the center of the village. The wall is much higher than a man, but stands in the yard of the smaller house and the red tiled roof of its larger neighbor begins its slope far above it. The small house is as modest as such houses can be, its own roof made of thatch. The big house is as grand as the scale of this village allows. Several steps climb up to its front door, so that the whole house is raised above the water from the monsoon rains that sometimes floods its neighbors.

The shape of the grand house is a cross. Four rooms are recessed from the center, resting in coolness and shade. The pillars as well as the beams are sky blue, and a column of light falls from an opening in the roof. It splashes into a shallow, dry well that is bordered by marble floors, the four sides decorated with the four symbols of playing cards. Air turns cool as it passes through the house, sheltered from the sun that blasts outside.

The Reddy family lives here, the parents and relatives of a young woman who stands to inherit it all. This young woman is an only child. Her inheritance will include more than two hundred acres of the finest land, for the young woman's family is the wealthiest that such an Indian village harbors.

There is a window in the wall behind their house. Behind it children stand and watch the comings and goings of their rich neighbors.

These children belong to a Reddy family too. Most of the people in these villages belong to a Reddy family. Reddy serves as a tribal or clan name, suggesting to which part of the country a family belongs rather than lineage. The land claims most of the villagers' lives. Dawn sees them rise and walk out to the fields, sunset sees them return home. Food is cooked over an open fire, for there is not yet electricity to help push day into night. The passing of the seasons and the growing and gathering of crops give rhythm to human life.

There is a clear link between the families on either side of the wall, though it is not one of blood relationship. One family is rich, the other poor. The rich Reddy family owns the land on which the poor Reddy family is paid to work.

They are not working on Christmas Day, 1960, however. The Christian holiday means nothing here and would pass unnoticed by those at work in the fields. Today, though, the young mother, Antamma, is in labor. She has two children already, a boy and a girl, but neither earlier pregnancy was as severe as this one is. She has already made the unusual and long trip over miles of dirt road to the nearest town to visit a hospital and consult a doctor.

Back in the village there is no medical assistance for the delivery, but neighbors come around to help. Water boils in a pot on a fire kept burning in the backyard. There are two small rooms partitioned off from the single room that constitutes the home. One is the shrine room dedicated to female deities. The other is used for storage and is cleared so that Antamma can lie in some privacy.

Her new baby is born in the early hours of December 26. The father recalls that the birth took place at six o'clock in the morning, though some remember it being four hours earlier. Antamma chooses a name for the child, a baby girl. She knows she is too weak from the birth to give the baby a mother's love and protection, for she needs all her strength to keep herself from dying. So she chooses a name that places the baby under the protection of the divine. The baby is named Kamala. The name bears the twin sacred meanings of "lotus" and "divine light."

There is no one to nurse her, so the baby's first food is the milk of a goat, poured into her mouth from a shell.

=◊=

KAMALA GROWS. She plays skipping games, she flies high on a swing strung from the branch of a tree, and she learns many songs, which she sings sweetly. The villagers enjoy having her among them and decide she is a good girl.

More children are born to the family, the fourth and fifth children girls and the sixth a boy. Kamala's sisters form a unit. Where one is working, the others move alongside. Tasks are shared, company is vital. Kamala can join them at any moment, for all moments. This is what sisters do, till life moves them into marriage.

Kamala is different. She finds a task and sets out to do it on her own. There is always a separate space somewhere, and Kamala occupies it.

In the daytime, when her child is between six and eight, Antamma sometimes walks with her into the forest. She spends the day collecting leaves to be sold for use as dinner plates in a large temple. While she works, Kamala finds a tree and sits beneath it. Sometimes Antamma works for just three hours, sometimes for the entire day, setting out at six in the morning and returning at eight at night. Kamala spends the time seated under a tree, neither moving nor uttering a word.

Back in the village at about this time a cow butts Kamala in the face, tearing out some of her hair with its horns, but she is otherwise unhurt and generally fearless.

She displays this lack of fear at night, as darkness falls and villagers return home for fear of unfamiliar solitude and of the snakes and scorpions that roam the paths. The villagers close themselves inside their homes, in the close-knit community that is always preferable to being alone, while Kamala walks her way back to the forest. She likes to sit within the hollow of a tree. The forest is there to enclose her and keep her company.

The frailty that came with her birth accompanies her through childhood. The strength that helped her survive remains with her too. The girl's slight body is frequently racked with violent pains. She shifts into unconsciousness for many hours at a time and her body is laid in the room where she was born. There is no doctor to be called. All the family can do is pray and wait for the off chance of recovery.

She does recover. The girl rises from her sickness each time and resumes her village life. Headaches sweep in to knock her down, fevers run so high that her wrists are too hot for her mother to touch, and she cries a lot with frequent attacks of pain. Death often seems very near. Near though it comes, so that its shadow falls over the girl's whole body, her urge for life is even stronger.

———◇———

A SCHOOL STANDS at an edge of the village. Its classroom faces a playing field of hard earth. Children come here for lessons up to the age of eleven. If their parents allow.

There are fewer girls than boys among the pupils. Kamala is not one of them. Veera, her father, cannot spare her for school. The family subsists on very little. Whatever the girl can add to their support is necessary. She has always helped where needed, and in the rice harvest it is noticed that the young girl's contribution is as much as a full-grown woman's. But now, at the age of eight, she is given a working role of her own.

The hours from dawn until dusk find her not in her small family home with its thatched roof, but in the grand house on the other side of the wall. In the world's eyes she is a servant, and the money for her work is added to her parents' wages. In her own view, little has changed. Instead of helping with the domestic duties in her family home, she helps another family. It is part of growing up. The transition from her family into a more independent life seems timely. It is an opening into a wider world she expects to become hers. She washes plates made of china instead of tin or leaf, helps care for saris made from fine silk instead of simple cotton, and learns to add exotic spices to more delicate food.

The grand household pines for two girls they have lost, a daughter and granddaughter who live far away. Their only daughter married when she was just nine years old. It was her father's idea, for he was very taken with the young man who appeared at his home gathering charitable donations for a boys' hostel. This young man, Venkat Reddy, came from a family of equivalent wealth. He had the right status and he was bright. The older man had always wanted such a son, and so arranged for Venkat to become his son-in-law. He intended to finance him through medical school so that he could return to the village as a doctor.

That was not to be. Venkat had no interest in the rigors of long-term study. He had twin passions, for a life of active social work and for direct contact with the leading spiritual figures of the day. Years passed and he carried away the family's daughter and their new granddaughter, Jyoti, aged four, to an ashram beside the Indian Ocean.

Kamala is bright and sensitive. She absorbs lessons just by watching. It is good and comforting to have another young girl around the house, and soon she is treated as a familiar. She is not expected to comment on what goes on in the family, but she hears it all as it passes about her.

Frequent letters come from the ashram, which is several days' journey away and so beyond the scope of family visits. The letters are read aloud and discussed, so that Kamala learns about Sri Aurobindo, the Indian sage and revolutionary around whom the ashram was founded. He died in 1950, but the ashram still holds a living figure at its core whom they consider divine. Her name is Mirra, also known as Sweet Mother or Mother Mirra. Now entering her nineties, she has ceased her regular appearances standing on a balcony to be viewed by devotees from below. Her presence is as vital to the ashram community as each member's beating heart. She is adored as a universal mother of all creation, a twin part of the divine incarnation on earth that received its first focus through the body of Sri Aurobindo.

Kamala hears of this divine mother. She also hears of Venkat. His mother-in-law and her sister rule this house where she spends every day. They were opposed to Venkat's marriage into their household from the beginning and are inclined to hear their prophecies of nuptial doom come true. They hear how he roams

the country on spiritual quests and consider this as abandonment
of his young family. They send money with their letters and fume
with the grievance that this will help fund Venkat's lifestyle. They
scan the letters from his wife for any signs of upset and debauch-
ery in his life and illuminate their guesswork with their imagina-
tions. There is a good side and a bad side to the man; they are
eager to hear more of the bad.

This distant man who is a passion in these elderly women's
lives is of interest to the girl. Kamala knows the local legends
about him, the stories of how he would approach any newborn
baby in search of signs of divinity. Two missions have been fixed
in him since childhood. They are his vocation, his divine calling.
He will find a child from his village whom he will promote to
world renown, and he will be the confidant and companion of the
supreme Divine Mother of the present age.

When he met the child he was to marry, he decided this was
that figure of his mission. When she refused to play along, he
looked elsewhere till his daughter, Jyoti, was born. This could be
that divine child. However, she grew up with a mind of her own
and was also reluctant.

Kamala senses her destiny in this man. His face takes substance in her visions and dreams.

She is eleven when Venkat's champion, the father of the
house, dies. Venkat is now forty-six. In July 1972, after years away,
he heads home to take charge of the estate. A woman and a girl
from the household walk the short distance down their lane to the
road that passes through their village and watch as he climbs
from the bus.

The girl is Kamala.

CHAPTER 5

The Mentor's Tale

In failing health, disheartened, the man who steps from the bus to the dust of the Indian village square is tired. The richness of his life seems trivial. The adventures of his life seem like escapes. The duties of home have claimed him at last, reeled him back in from his dreams of a special place in the wider world.

Soon the man will be returned to the excitements of his childhood.

———◇———

AMMA IS THE WORD in his language for "mother" and the young Venkat's distinctive call. "*Amma,*" he says, tears rolling down his face, a cry of loss and longing. "*Amma.*"

His own mother cannot comfort him. Even in her arms, his cry for *Amma* continues. This *Amma* of his childhood longing is no regular mother. She is God on earth, the divine in a tender female form. Since the age of four he knows that his mission in life is to find such a being and be her primary companion and aid.

And her best-loved child.

He does not yet know that this mission will take him forty-two years to accomplish.

"*Amma.*"

⸺◇⸺

As A CHILD, Venkat has no great love of reading or study and prefers his own silent company to the company of playmates. Children come to be with him at his parents' large family home. They sit in a circle around him and wait there till he gives them a piece of candy, so they will go and leave him alone. He knows that one day he will discover the child he is destined to bring to the attention of the whole world. He feels no call for the companionship of lesser children than this.

Of more interest than going to school is founding a school of his own. In 1941, before he is sixteen years old, he has collected enough funds to establish a hostel for boys in the nearby town of Borngiri, and he continues to collect enough contributions to pay for all of its operating costs through the years to come. Full board and education are provided for about one hundred boys at a time.

⸺◇⸺

VENKAT'S SEARCH for charitable funds with which to maintain the hostel takes him to the village of Chandepalle, where he heads for the biggest house in town.

The head of the household has one child, a daughter. In Venkat he sees the model of the son he would have liked to have had, a boy who would grow up, train to become a doctor, and bring his skills back to his home village. While he cannot adopt Venkat as his son, he can acquire him as his son-in-law. Marriage with his daughter is arranged, with the understanding that Venkat will accept funding through medical school.

Venkat has no real interest in the long, rigorous course of study needed to become a doctor, and so that plan is soon dropped. He is intent on being of service right now rather than at some time in the future.

His new wife has a clear view of her marriage. Her new husband is handsome, while she is "plain and dark with lots of land."

She is also only nine years old. She and her husband come from similar backgrounds as far as wealth and social standing go, but he is more than double her age. A young child is married to a man, one who is eager to pit himself against a wider world.

Upon his marriage Venkat surrenders his share in his own family's land, a portion of about fifty acres, to his three brothers. Soon after this he heads out into India with a friend, Naram Reddy, from his new child-wife's village. They are on a social mission to do good.

The two of them move off to the ashram of Mahatma Gandhi at Varda, north of Bombay. This ashram provides an example of village life as a model of much that is best in India. The ashram attracts many of the country's leading political figures. While there, the two young men from Chandepalle meet with Rajianbao, the first president of the newly formed republic of India.

From this ashram Venkat sets off to wander through his homeland with Vinobha Bhave. Among Gandhi's colleagues and associates, some continue his legacy in the political dimension, but Vinobha takes Gandhi's principles as the calling of his life. Taking no home as his own, he sets off on a mission through the villages of all India. This mission is called the Bhoodan tour, the land-gift movement. It involves constant travel, frequently with walks of forty kilometers a day. The objective is to persuade those with large tracts of land to set aside some acres as a gift for the poor who have no land at all. He needs men and women to walk with him, people with their own individual powers of persuasion and stamina. Vinobha Bhave has sworn to continue the tour for as long as his life and his legs hold out, and for months at a time Venkat walks with him. It is a period of strenuous excitement, considerable success, and little sleep.

Vinobha grows fond of Venkat, calling him "mother" in appreciation of the care this younger man bestows on him and those around him. He gives Venkat his best advice.

"Give up love of money and love of women," Vinobha tells him. "Then you'll be great."

Vinobha assigns Venkat three acres of land on which to start an ashram, in the town of Manchiralla. Set beside the Brodari River, it is dedicated to social service and the provision of hospitals and schools. Naram joins Venkat there. They plant coconut trees and crops, start the buildings and the kindergarten, power the complex with an oil generator, and spend some years building and maintaining the ashram.

———◇———

VENKAT MAKES REGULAR JOURNEYS out to a hilltop some hours west of Hyderabad in his home state of Andhra Pradesh, where a holy woman lives.

This woman spends most of her life closed away in a hut on the hill. Her name is Mannikyamma. Once a year, on the annual occasion of the festival of Shivatri, she breaks from her state of deep union with God and steps out from the hut so that devotees can see her. The sight of such a holy woman helps develop their spiritual growth.

A woman who contents herself with the life of an anchoress, closed up in a hut with only the barest amounts of food and drink, is not in urgent need of Venkat. She nevertheless welcomes him and is happy for him to stay. He helps erect the wooden buildings of her ashram but needs more from the person who will be his divine mother.

His need for a divine mother is growing desperate. If he cannot find such a being to give him some sense of himself, he will have to kill himself. There is nothing else he can think to do with the life he has been given. A friend notes his desperation and suggests that he visit a woman known as Anadhoota Chinnamma.

Chinnamma lives in Repali, in the Krishna District of Andhra Pradesh. With a shaven head, she sits naked beneath the loose drapings of a cotton sheet, for any clothing set against her skin burns to nothing.

Venkat is twenty-eight when he finds her. He stays with her for two years, writing many letters to friends. He wants them to come and see the glory that he has found for himself. This is the closest he has yet come to finding the mother of his longing, and he feels that the understanding and knowledge that are the power of the scriptures become his just through sitting in her presence. He is allowed to stay by her side night and day.

Chinnamma sometimes grows exasperated with Venkat. "You shouldn't stay because you are not listening," she tells him.

Venkat goes off to speak about Chinnamma at a meeting in Madras. There are those there who speak with passion of another divine mother, Sweet Mother of Pondicherry. He hears their passion, hears a quality of confidence in it that is surer than his own, and suddenly he knows. Chinnamma is a woman of marvelous goodness and power, but even she recognizes his dissatisfaction and tells him he will only be satisfied with the supreme Divine Mother of the present age. He leaves the meeting and moves on to visit Sweet Mother at Pondicherry, hoping that she is just such a being.

Sweet Mother has dedicated her own life to serving someone she takes to be the most supreme divine being ever born on earth—Sri Aurobindo. He kept to his rooms in this Indian seaside town, writing his works of spiritual philosophy and making his visionary journeys through different spiritual planes, while devotees gathered around him. Sweet Mother took the force of their devotion and fashioned it into a highly organized and extensive ashram. Sri Aurobindo died in 1950, but Sweet Mother has lived on as the focus of the ashram's devotional life.

Once there, Venkat succumbs to devotion himself.

He returns to Chinnamma and asks her permission to leave her. She grants it, and he moves on to stay with his new mother, Sweet Mother of Pondicherry.

———◇———

VENKAT'S DAUGHTER, JYOTI, is four years old when he takes her and his wife from their village to Sweet Mother and the Aurobindo ashram. Jyoti cries on the way there, desperately unhappy when she finds that they are not going to stay with the holy woman called Chinnamma. She has heard so much of this fine woman from her father and only wants to be with her.

They arrive at the ashram and are met by a man named Dara. He came to Aurobindo's ashram in the 1920s, bringing with him just three dhotis, simple stretches of cotton cloth to wrap around himself as clothing. Behind him he left the wealth and position that were his as a son of the great ruling Nawab family of Hyderabad. He is a visionary and tells the newcomers of a vision he has just received.

The image is of a woman, wrapped loosely in cotton cloth and with a shaven head. In his vision she comes to Sweet Mother and asks leave to go to Nirvana. This is the state of great bliss beyond the turmoil of life, and all who wish for it have to gain Sweet Mother's permission. Sweet Mother says no, but the woman persists, saying she does not want to be part of the world anymore. When Sweet Mother finally relents, the shaven-headed woman zooms off like a rocket.

"Yes, we know such a woman," Venkat admits when asked.

A letter is already on its way to him at the ashram telling him of Chinnamma's death.

———◇———

SWEET MOTHER is a very old and celebrated woman when Venkat arrives at her ashram. In a young Frenchman called Sat Prem she already has a confidant of her own. Sat Prem has the type of intimacy Venkat yearns for. Sweet Mother has command of a substantial and wealthy ashram that she herself has built. The institution is focused through its reverence for her. There are others within the ashram structure who are very close to her, but Sat Prem is a renegade outsider in whom she puts her confidence.

Later on, as she enters her nineties, as her body becomes too weak to defend itself, she will share thoughts with Sat Prem about the possibilities of eternal life. If just one cell of her body can be rendered totally divine, and therefore eternal, then the whole fabric of creation will be changed. No more tremendous step in the spiritual maturation of the universe can be achieved. Aurobindo died before he could complete the task, which she is carrying on within her own body.

Sat Prem will be taken with her ideas, though others in the ashram will deem them to be senile. They would prefer that she allow herself simply to be worshiped as a goddess, which she will resist. In the last months of her life, the old woman and her young compatriot friend will be kept apart. Sweet Mother will feel the lack of appreciation for her endeavors to have her body live forever and so will let herself die. She will claim she will rest in her tomb till someone comes along who is capable of valuing her work for what it is.

On arrival at the Aurobindo ashram, Venkat attempts to introduce his own young wife into the ashram as a new divine mother, but the attempt founders. The young woman loves fairy tales and the stories of gods, an interest she will maintain throughout her adult life, but she feels no need to live in a fairy tale of her own. She has an education. She has some wealth and land and a fine home. She has a handsome, charismatic husband. She is content to enjoy it all and does not need to trade it in for some fantasy about her own special divinity.

For the present, Sweet Mother is the best divine mother available. There is nowhere else for Venkat to be. However, he is too late on a crowded scene to claim the special relationship he needs.

Instead of staying in the ashram, he continues his search for holy people elsewhere and carries photographs of Sweet Mother to give to all he meets along the way. In the villages of Nalgonda, his home district, he is Sweet Mother's only apostle.

In 1956 Jyoti and her mother receive Sweet Mother's permission to become permanent residents of the ashram. Venkat takes his daughter to visit friends, proud to declare that she is a child of the ashram, and asks them to give money for her education. Since education at the ashram is free, these funds support his continual wandering through India in search of its holy men and women, while spreading the word and the teachings of Aurobindo and Sweet Mother.

In 1968, some twelve years after installing his wife and child, he settles into a more stable ashram life, taking on the twin jobs of teaching Telugu and working as a receptionist by the front gate.

Many will come to remember him with great affection for his acts of kindness, especially young women who awake in him a special fondness. They come to the ashram gates at a loss from problems in the outside world, distraught with the situation in which they find themselves. He is the first person they see. He takes them in hand and finds them a role to play in ashram life until the routine and the spiritual air of the ashram restore them to some sense of calm.

The fact that almost every one of those whose lives he helps so much is a young woman lands Venkat in trouble. The families of the girls frequently come looking for their daughters and their sisters and challenge the role of protector he has assumed in their lives. He accepts their abuse and waits for them to go away. Whenever the next troubled young woman arrives at the ashram gates, he welcomes her in.

=◇=

BACK IN ANDHRA PRADESH the holy man known as Sai Baba, the most revered such figure in all India, is already drawing large crowds to his ashram at Puttaparthi. Venkat engages Sai Baba in conversation in the ashram's coconut grove and is proud to report Sai Baba's annoyance when attendants come to call him away to another engagement.

This holy man is a good model for his young daughter, Jyoti, Venkat decides. He takes her with him on a visit.

"See!" her father tells her. "Do you see how many followers Sai Baba has? If you are good, you can have as many followers as he does."

He gives the young girl many spiritual books to read and tells her she should become Krishna Meera.

Krishna Meera was a sixteenth-century Indian saint, a princess and a poet who defied convention and rejoiced in spiritual communion with what her royal family thought of as the rabble who sang the god Krishna's praises. When chased by her persecutors, she merged into a statue of Krishna, leaving him draped in her clothes. Her songs are widely loved still. They are some of Venkat's favorite music.

Jyoti, however, does not want to be Meera.

"Why don't you be Krishna?" she asks her father.

——◇——

"Why don't you be Krishna?"

It is a retort more than it is a question, but there is an answer. Divinity rests in every human being, waiting to be recognized. It is sparked into existence when it is seen. Venkat can be Krishna for Jyoti only if she is prepared to see such divine qualities in him. She adamantly refuses to see him in this light.

The sun draws saltwater from the Indian Ocean to leave it hanging in the air. There are no sea breezes to make life pleasant in the summer streets of Pondicherry, simply the moisture packed as humidity inside the heat. Fans move some air through the ashram houses, but for now the electricity has failed. Jyoti as a young girl lies in bed and sweats with the fever of an illness. Her father sits beside her bed throughout the night, fanning her to keep her cool.

Many speak of Venkat's great love for his daughter. She feels the love, but comes to believe he only loves her as his own reflection. She feels an intense need for a clear identity of her own. When she agrees with her father, he praises her. When she disagrees with him he announces, "That's your mother in you who's speaking now." She wants space to grow into her own view of herself.

Venkat has no one else to turn to in his search for someone prepared to become his special divine mother. For several years he leads a calmer life, an ashram life harnessed to devotion and routine. He rises at four o'clock every morning. For hours before dawn and again at sunset he meditates beside the tomb of Sri Aurobindo, knowing that Sweet Mother is in her room up above. For his hours of work he moves away a few yards to sit beside the main gates of the ashram, an official receptionist for those who come to visit. Three times a week he also works as a teacher, giving classes in Telugu for young people in the ashram's school.

His longing to promote a child from his village and to be the primary companion of a divine mother does not diminish. He has simply exhausted his pilgrimage in the outer world. He knows nowhere else to look, nowhere else to go. Surrender is part of being still. Venkat turns his journey inward and opens to whatever force might come from Sweet Mother.

The years in which he keeps to the Aurobindo ashram and does not return to his wife's estate coincide with the years that Kamala is working in his house there.

On the death of his father-in-law, Venkat leaves his wife and daughter in their ashram home and returns to his village with some sense of failure. Later in life Mother Meera will look back and recall the romance of this moment, when as the girl Kamala she first looks on Venkat and he on her. He is the man of her own visions, in his clean white Indian clothes and his trim white cap. He stands on the lower step of the bus as it stops on the village street, holds on to the railing, and stares into her eyes. He cannot climb down, cannot move, cannot blink, but only stare.

"Who is this girl?" he asks, and when he learns that she is the servant in his household, he hands her his suitcase to carry.

The face of the young girl matches the face that was part of his vision forty years before, the vision of the child he would promote from his village to a position of world renown. He knows as soon as he sees her at the bus stand that this is the girl that his life has been drawing him toward, but he has grown cautious. After all, he once felt he knew the same about his child-wife and daughter, that these girls would grow into the divine mother of his dream.

He watches Kamala, speaks with her, keeps her in his company as much as he can. When she is sent away against his wishes, as temporary help in the household of a Sikh family in Hyderabad, a full day's journey away, her absence creates a hollow in his life.

This is the point at which the divinity of Mother Meera is first recognized within the young girl Kamala. The scene is so important in the story of Mother Meera that it has been much embellished in the latest authorized account, included in *Answers Part 2* (1997). Embellishments include the appearance of Kamala to Venkat in physical form though she is miles away. This apparition of Kamala is so real that she is able to take food from Venkat's hand and advise him of the nature of his own divinity.

In the undoctored version of the story, Venkat is lying on his bed in his village home one evening, asleep, when he hears her call. He jumps up and chases the memory of the voice around the house, but cannot find her. Sometime later he makes the journey to Hyderabad to visit her. She asks why he did not hear her when she came to him, why he did not notice anything. He now understands she truly was with him when he felt her to be there, but asks how it was possible. The distance between them was too great for her to have bridged it on her own.

"There are other ways of traveling," she tells him.

Now he knows. This is the girl that forty-two years of his quest have prepared him to serve.

WHEN KAMALA WAS SIX YEARS OLD she stepped on a thorn. Two centimeters long, it entered through the sole of her foot and pierced the top. The family tried herbal remedies, but nobody was able to pull or coax the thorn out. The nearest doctor was in the town of Borngiri, thirty-five kilometers away, but there was no transport to get there.

Veera hoisted his daughter onto his shoulders while his wife, Antamma, walked by his side, soothing the girl as she cried. They walked all the way to town, waited through a successful operation to remove the thorn, then carried the girl the thirty-five kilometers of the return journey.

The extreme difficulty of this visit to the doctor is one measure of the girl's isolation. Villages like Kamala's survive by being self-sufficient. Illness meets with recovery or death, for there is usually no medical support within the village. The only assistance villagers have to call on is the help of the gods, and in times of emergency they turn to prayer.

Kamala's family enjoys making one particular excursion out of their village. When the opportunity arises, they sit on a bullock cart and are carried off on a day's pilgrimage. They are lucky in that one of the foremost temples is southern India is situated in their district. Set on a small hill that rises from a plain, its walls are white and dazzle in the sunlight. Monkeys patrol the perimeter looking for banana offerings.

The temple is dedicated to the god Lakshman Narayan. Its interior is largely one main ceremonial hall, spacious and filled with light. The principal idol is a jolly one. Made of silver, he is like a monster from some animated Eastern cartoon, a monster who only growls because it is expected of him, but truly has a heart of gold. Saucer eyes bulge from his lionlike head, and his body is held so as to form a silver throne with his lap as the seat. His left arm curves around to protect a small silver figure of a goddess that stands in his embrace.

—◇—

VENKAT SEEKS TO STRETCH THE ARM of his own protection around the young girl. It is not easy. Venkat's mother-in-law and her sister remember tales of him as a boy. He used to hurry to get sight of any new baby born in the district. He looked into each baby's eyes for signs of divinity, proclaiming that the newborn child was "a good boy" or "a good girl" and would grow up to be at least a government minister. They remember how he tried to turn his own wife and daughter into divine mothers. Now here he is, back in their household and investing their servant girl with notions of divinity. They are upset with Venkat's need to have the girl at his side from dawn, when she arrives at his house, to dusk, when she returns to her family. This not only goes against their social and moral codes, it deprives them of help in the house.

The girl too seems to be taking her employer's words to heart.

"I can't work like other people," she tells her uncle, the first person in her family to hear the secret of her divinity from her own lips. "Many people will come and visit me."

A compromise is reached. Kamala will spend certain hours of certain days of the week on her work and is free on the other days to spend time with Venkat.

—◇—

WE LEAVE THE VILLAGE of Chandepalle behind us, follow a raised track that runs for a couple of kilometers across the fields of the plain, and pause just before we reach the outer trees of the forest. We have followed Venkat away from the domestic maelstrom of life in the village house and into the relative peace of his alternate home.

A large well is located just outside the walls of this home. Some twenty feet in diameter, it plunges deep to whatever water can be found. The richness of the land, the crops, and the orchards stem from this well. Trees grow high to spread shade across the cluster of farm buildings. Red brick walls form the framework, reaching out at right angles from a long rear wall, and the spaces between them are filled in as needed. Some spaces are built into barns, some into cowsheds, but the first we come to is divided into rooms that constitute Venkat's farmhouse.

Mangoes drop from the trees and cattle, goats, and geese enliven the place with their noise and their smells, but for Venkat this is a pastoral setting more than it is a farm. A seed was sown when he met Kamala. The seed is their relationship, and the relationship is formed from recognition. There are two parts to the seed, each of which needs to grow as a balance to the other.

The first part is Venkat's recognition of Kamala's status as a supreme divine being. There is as yet no other person who accepts that this is the girl's nature. This recognition must spread from Venkat to those around him and then to all they meet, on and on till the whole world is touched by this recognition.

The other part involves Kamala's accepting this recognition of her divine status and taking steps to meet the demands such a recognition places upon her. Until now her divine nature has been a secret she kept to herself. She has a personal history, an inner autobiography she has related to nobody, accounts of an inner life that has also been a cosmic life. Her story is colored by the characters and effects of Hindu lore, inhabited by gods and goddesses and mythic beasts, and it tells of the girl's education in celestial spaces. She has spoken to no one of such events, which her family simply viewed as severe physical illness that often bordered on death and left her unconscious.

This first occurred at the age of six, when Kamala lay senseless for a whole day. Mother Meera declares that while her outer form changes, she is actually subject to no development. As an adult she is exactly the same as she was as a child, and indeed as she was before birth. However, her own account of her life story tells

of a spiritual evolution. It is this experience of a day's seeming unconsciousness at the age of six that teaches her complete detachment from all human relationships. At the age of two or three she
remembers going to "different lights" for her education. As she
tells these stories to Venkat, these "lights" take on the identities of
various Indian deities and other figures, but in infancy she has
not yet acquired such cultural terms of reference.

While her grandfather has been happy to come to the young
girl for advice, there has been no one who could accept her full
story as other than fantasy. Now Venkat comes along with an eagerness to credit each of her tales as a divine experience.

The greatest gift that Venkat can give her is his belief in her.
This really is the incarnation of the being who will be brought to
the world's attention as Mother Meera, for it is the moment when
the consciousness of her divine nature passes into humanity.

Venkat accepts the girl as a supreme divine being. For once, to
his utmost relief, he finds a girl who is eager to accept all he proclaims her to be. Little by little she tells him details from the story
of her divine mission to earth, a story never hinted at to anyone
before Venkat draws it from her. He extends his protection so that
she can grow into her public role. His acceptance of her as a divine mother moves her from a private into a public mode. The
world will love her and it will also mock her for entering into such
a relationship with it. To survive in such a world, she first has to
develop the strongest sense of her own divine nature.

Kamala's recognition of her own divine role takes its strength
from Venkat's recognition of the divine in her and the intensity of
his wish to see her in such a divine role. She now has to give expression to her sense of her own supreme divinity, something
that she has so far kept a secret from the world.

The visions and dreams she describes to Venkat are the first
articulation of this awareness of divinity. Mother Meera is known
for silence, but in these early years her existence is defined

through her relationship with Venkat Reddy, and much of this relationship consists of the talk that passes between them.

Some of this talk is recorded in *The Mother*, a book by Adilakshmi that contains many of Venkat's verbatim reports of the young Mother Meera's dreams and visionary experiences. We only hear one side of this dialogue in the book. Within the Aurobindo ashram Venkat had a considerable reputation as an interpreter of dreams and visions, using Aurobindo's philosophy as a base from which to extend mystical significance to a dream's episodes. Kamala has received no formal education at all. Venkat now provides it. He helps her give voice to her experience, and in helping to formulate this experience in terms of story he gives it the scope to develop. Kamala's experiences shift from the unconscious to the conscious, from the inexpressible to the expressed, in the same way her body learns to incorporate the trance state into the more regular moments of her physical life. She is learning to bridge the material and immaterial worlds.

Most of us do this to some degree. We harbor aspirations as we move through our more hard-edged life and escape into passages of fantasy and prayer from time to time. For Kamala, removal from the physical to the spiritual world is no longer optional. Her openness to the divine, her access to realms of spirit, her existence as a cosmic force have to be constant and conscious; they have to infuse every moment of her existence on earth. Venkat's awareness of her potential requires this of her. It magnetizes her potential into complete existence. It molds her into his dream image of all a divine mother can be.

━━◇━━

KAMALA'S PARENTS, Veera and Antamma, are slow to appreciate the idea that their daughter should now be given the respect due to a goddess. To them it seems suspicious that their boss should want to keep their young daughter by his side all the time, day and night if possible.

Venkat spends a great deal of time with two of his employees, the watchman of the estate and his wife. He brings his position and his powers of persuasion to bear on the couple, until they are the first people after him to accept Kamala's divinity.

He then leaves the couple to work alongside their best friends and fellow employees, Kamala's parents.

"She is divine," Veera and Antamma hear from their best friends, Veera out in the fields and Antamma over the laundry. "Kamala is divine. Your daughter is divine."

Eventually, they come to believe that it is true.

——◇——

ALL IS NOT SO SIMPLE back in the village house. There is an argument, and Venkat's mother-in-law's sister slaps Kamala across the face. The girl walks out and away from her work. When Venkat hears the news, he hurries to find her.

She is carrying a basketload of dung off to the rice fields.

"Why are you here?" he asks her. "Don't do this work. You are the Divine Mother."

A version of the goddess Lakshmi, whose name, like Mother Meera's own given name of Kamala, evokes the lotus, is the tutelary deity of India's rice-growing areas. She is known as "The One Possessing Dung." Carrying dung in a rice field is a perfect condition for a Hindu divine mother, who has all the attributes of all creation as part of her being.

However, Kamala accepts Venkat's counsel and goes off with him to his farmhouse, where she spends several days.

Offended at the assault on their daughter by their employers, her parents resign the jobs they have held for five years. In time they will return for one more year's employment on the Reddy estate, but for now they have to earn a more precarious living by hiring themselves out as temporary labor.

Without her own work as a servant, Kamala is now free to spend more time at the farmhouse. She begins to sleep there and wakes in the night to dictate her visions to Venkat. Her family sometimes walks out to visit her, as do some villagers. They sit in the courtyard while she is in trance, careful not to disturb her, then move away with a sense of blessing.

※

BACK IN PONDICHERRY the Aurobindo ashram is going through the severest of times. In 1973 Sweet Mother dies. She has been the ashram's gathering and organizing vital force for many years. The loss of her living presence is felt extremely.

One woman at the ashram has come close to ending her own life, so troubled is she by the loss of Sweet Mother. She is sustained by letters sent to her by her friend Venkat Reddy. The letters tell of a new divine mother, a young girl called Kamala he has discovered in his own village home. He reports that upon Sweet Mother's death he saw her *shakti*, her divine powers, fly from her to enter this young girl. The woman must be strong, must endure until he brings Kamala to meet her.

The woman is Adilakshmi.

After two years in Chandepalle together, Kamala goes away with Venkat from the village of her birth to the Mahbubnagar ashram in the west of her home state of Andhra Pradesh. She spends some time there in preparation for her presentation at the Aurobindo ashram in the seaside city of Pondicherry.

One of the first people she meets there is Adilakshmi. Now aged thirty, Adilakshmi has lived an unconventional life. As she meets with the young girl Kamala, the wondrous events of her own journey through life begin to make sense.

CHAPTER 6

The Handmaid's Tale

Adilakshmi Olati's hometown of Madanapalle lies just a little inside the southwestern border of Andhra Pradesh in southern India. It is a hill region, so its temperature in summer is some ten degrees cooler than in other areas of the state. The climate attracts many visitors to the Olati home, including several of the leading political and spiritual figures of the day. Adilakshmi is allowed to spend time with them.

Adilakshmi's father was a notable independence fighter in India's struggle for freedom from British rule. When armed soldiers stormed into his room he stood up, ripped open his shirt to bare his chest, and shouted his challenge into their faces. "Shoot me!"

He uses the same fiery qualities to power his family and his business life. With nine children and a retail clothing business on the town's main street, there is enough to keep him busy.

One of his daughters provides a special challenge.

Adilakshmi is born on July 13, 1943. She is a happy child, although it baffles her to find herself born into such a family as the Olatis. Her true family isn't this tangle of human emotions, love, dependency, and needs. Hers is a divine family that she will meet somewhere beyond the confines of her home.

In the meantime she will teach her birth family a better way of living. Whenever her parents argue, the young girl goes on a hunger strike. She refuses to eat until the argument is officially resolved in front of her.

<hr />

HER ACADEMIC RECORD at school is average, though her headmistress takes such special care of her that Adilakshmi calls her "*Amma,*" the term in her own language of Telugu for "mother."

Her move to the university is a great liberation—away from the family home to a girls' hostel on campus. She attends the Venkateswara University of Tirupati, a few hours' drive southeast from her home, to study home economics.

The same journey from Madanapalle to Tirupati was made some millennia before hers by one of India's most powerful gods. Two pointed hills are stationed on either side of the town of Madanapalle, and legend tells of how the god Venkateswara strode above the town using the hills as stepping stones. These simple few strides brought him to the hills of Tirupati, where he chose to settle and make his home.

The university campus is spread across the plain directly below the sacred hills of Tirupati. At sunset a string of lamps lights the first stretch of the pilgrims' footpath mounting the hillside toward the monumental arch set on the first ridge. Adilakshmi sits by her window at night and looks out at the lights—they are almost reflected in her eyes as she pauses to remember them in a room in Germany later in life.

"I always see God outside," she muses. "Never inside."

=◇=

In 1962–63 India wages war with China, and Adilakshmi jumps onto a bus filled with male students to join a march through the streets. "Give money for the war!" she shouts, rattling her collection box at passers-by.

She likes to be at the center of attention and enjoys acting on stage. In the university's drama groups she specializes in comedy.

After graduating she moves on to postgraduate work, taking an M.A. in philosophy. A young professor is assigned to tutor his first group of students, including Adilakshmi. She listens to him, watches him, and decides that he is her destiny. Adilakshmi confides to a student friend that she and the professor will marry. Knowing nothing of this intention, the young professor devastates Adilakshmi by marrying someone else.

Adilakshmi is seen as a conscientious and competent though not outstanding student. It is felt that she will follow the path expected of most of the female students—that she will make a good marriage and bear children.

Tutors note her tendency toward "spiritual" rather than "philosophical" concerns. However, one lecturer from her undergraduate program is always happy to have Adilakshmi visit her home. She and her doctor husband note the benefits such a visit generally brings. Whatever difficulties they are undergoing in their lives, a solution follows Adilakshmi's visit. She does nothing to actively bring about such a change; it is simply a grace that follows her presence.

After six years at the university it is no longer possible to settle back into family life at Madanapalle. Adilakshmi has known since childhood that one day she will leave to join an ashram. Now, in the summer of 1969, it seems that the time has arrived.

She leaves a note for her family.

"I am leaving home and joining an ashram."

She does not yet know which ashram, so she can say nothing more.

———◇———

ADILAKSHMI TAKES NO BELONGINGS or clothes from her home, in the belief that God will provide for her. She takes just one hundred rupees and sets out through the door.

A companion throughout Adilakshmi's childhood was a small statue of the holy man Sai Baba of Shirdi. The figure was like a grandfather who offered wisdom, comfort, and understanding. She liked to sleep alone because others would not understand how she needed to talk to her small statue, to tell it the intimacies of her life before sleeping with it by her side. She vowed to visit this saint's shrine before moving on into the next stage of her life.

In the mid-nineteenth century Sai Baba appeared in the small town of Shirdi, a present-day car trip of around nine hours north from Bombay. He made his home in a mosque there and stayed until his death in 1918. The image of this bearded sage, a white bandanna tied around his head and his right hand raised in a blessing, is found throughout India and held in great reverence.

The saint's origins are mysterious; no one even knows his original name. Sai means "saint" and Baba "father." He taught through whatever religion seekers brought to him, applying either miracles, common sense, or a slap of the hand as needed to awaken his followers to their full spiritual dimension.

Adilakshmi's journey to visit him is a long one. On the arduous train trip she sees herself protected in her compartment by the presence of lions and tigers.

In Bombay she spends the night in a dormitory for pilgrims. It is very dark, she is the only female among crowds of men, and she feels very uncomfortable. She complains to her "grandfather," to Sai Baba, the way she used to as a child: "This is not fair. I come all this way to see you and you leave me alone in a place like this. You should give me some protection."

Immediately she feels the security of a response.

Before leaving Madanapalle she was preparing special food in the family kitchen, having heard within herself the cry, "*Amma, give me food.*"

Once the food was prepared, the call she had anticipated duly came; it came in the same voice as had sounded within her, with the same words, in the same tones. She stepped out of the house to find a huge man waiting for her, very dark and with a shiny face. Instead of the leftover food usually given to beggars, she brought out all her special dishes and laid the banquet before him on the lawn, standing back and feeling very happy as she watched him eat.

Now she sees the same man, with the same shiny face, walking around the perimeter of the room. She knows he is there to guard her and that she is safe.

The next day there is no special train to Shirdi, which lies on a branch line from the main railway line that sweeps northeast. As Adilakshmi waits at the station a special chartered train comes through with its load of pilgrims from the holy city of Benares. They see the lone woman in her white sari on the platform and invite her to travel with them for free.

It is a long and hot journey, and when Adilakshmi arrives at their destination she complains again.

"Shirdi Baba, Grandfather, I have come all this way to see you and I am hungry, yet there is nothing for me to eat."

The pilgrims spread out a feast and invite their new friend to join them. Adilakshmi recognizes the conclusion of her trip and thanks Shirdi Sai Baba deeply. When she enters the shrine and meets the shining marble statue of the great saint sitting above his tomb, it is a great and powerful homecoming.

——◇——

THE PILGRIMS FROM BENARES are continuing their journey to Pandaripur and Krishna's birthplace and invite Adilakshmi to come along with them. This involves a journey by bus to a railway station where she waits in line to buy her ticket. When she has paid her money she looks at the ticket she has bought. Instead of Pandaripur, it says Pondicherry. Remembering the ticket line, she realizes this was what her mouth unwittingly asked for and so accepts this new destination and carries on alone.

She has to change trains at Villapuram and wait for a connection to carry her down the branch line to the coast. This is the station where Ramana Maharshi, one of the twentieth century's most beloved holy figures, set off on his journey to the sacred mountain Arunachala. His teaching was largely in silence, but its essence is contained in three words, "Who am I?" He gives people the instruction to keep asking themselves the question, chasing the answer until it leads them to the true source of their being.

A policeman approaches Adilakshmi on the platform at Villapuram station.

"Who are you?" he asks.

Amused by the question, by its echo of Ramana Maharshi, Adilakshmi takes it as a sign that her quest is on the right track.

—◇—

THOUGH SHE IS FRESH from a master's degree in philosophy, Adilakshmi knows nothing of the Indian philosopher Sri Aurobindo. The only encounter she remembers is with a photograph that hung on the walls of her philosophy department, his name misspelled.

Born in East India to an Anglophile father who had the task of raising both his sons as a single parent, Aurobindo was sent as an eight-year-old boy to Britain. The boy who arrived in that damp climate spoke English as his native language and did not return to India until after his university education.

As his boat approached Bombay, he felt himself enveloped for the first time by what he would come to recognize as a spiritual dimension. His first acts, though, were ones of political rebellion;

he used the skills acquired during his British education to give the Indian movement for independence from Britain one of its foremost voices, advocating armed uprisings. His fight for his country's freedom was simultaneously a fight for his own, and he embarked on a program of study to read Indian literature and learn Indian languages.

He married and had a child, but in the thrust of his biography these are seen as incidentals. The British authorities imprisoned him, and experiences in the solitude of his prison cell helped him shift from a political to a spiritual perspective.

Upon his release he headed for the French protectorate of Pondicherry, where the British legal system could not reach him, and declined further part in the battle for India's independence. He now had all the personal independence he needed, and he settled into a suite of rooms he would seldom leave till his death. He had begun his study of what he would term "integral yoga," drawn from his own experience of mystical realms, and began work on a vast body of literature that would form one of the century's most complete expositions of the spiritual condition.

His writings on yoga draw on the many centuries of Indian spiritual tradition, then use this Hindu platform to launch a new understanding. This yoga accepts the nature of divine grace, that the spiritual path is not simply the release of the essence of God from within but an opening to the inrush of God through the crown of the head and into the body.

His most complete tome on the subject is *The Life Divine*, though a more accessible introduction is provided by his *Letters on Yoga*, a collection of letters written in response to devotees' questions.

In later years a devotee of Mother Meera will ask her if all the experiences he is receiving on his path with her, experiences he has just found described in Aurobindo's writings and ones he has never known on any other path, are in fact Aurobindo's integral yoga.

"Of course," Mother Meera will reply.

Aurobindo never chose to have devotees. They simply gathered around him and refused to leave. When a French woman and her husband came on a visit, this situation would change.

Born of Turkish and Egyptian parents, this woman had had an exotic life. She had mixed with the leaders of the French art movements of her time and spent a considerable period studying the occult in Egypt. Her meeting with Aurobindo was her meeting with destiny. She shed her husband and returned to Pondicherry. In her new role as "Sweet Mother," she formed half of what would be deemed a whole, one incarnation in two bodies, Sri Aurobindo and herself.

They both worked on the spiritual plane, gave spiritual discourses, and avowed the same mission, but while Aurobindo concerned himself with his writings and subsequent silence, she took the gathering devotees in hand and began to mold what would grow into a powerful and wealthy spiritual community dedicated to putting the messages of Sri Aurobindo's philosophy into practice.

Sri Aurobindo died in 1950 and was buried in the ashram's central courtyard. Sweet Mother still lives there as Adilakshmi draws close.

———◇———

ADILAKSHMI ARRIVES in Pondicherry at noon, just a few days short of her twenty-sixth birthday, which will fall on July 13, 1969. It is a time of day and a time of year when the sky is like a lens that intensifies the heat of the sun. The air is baked and barely suitable for breathing.

Adilakshmi makes her way toward the Sri Aurobindo ashram and pauses in the street outside. Its walls are high and its buildings grand. It is an institution so much vaster than the simple group of huts she was expecting that she does not know how to approach it. She looks at the women around her in their clean white saris, then looks down at her own made grimy by three days of travel. With her uncombed hair she knows she must look wild and doubts that she will be allowed inside.

There was a famous film actor in her native state, one who always played the part of a villain, who was her dear favorite as a girl. She loved to see his picture on posters around her hometown and would make sure to see every one of his movies as it appeared. Here, dressed immaculately in white and waiting in the shade of a tree, is a man so like that actor that she feels she recognizes him. They meet for this first time and it is as though they are already old and dear acquaintances.

The man is Venkat Reddy. He teaches their shared native language of Telugu in the ashram school on Mondays, Wednesdays, and Fridays. Thinking the day is Wednesday, he is waiting for his students. The day is in fact Tuesday. He is a punctual and punctilious man who never makes a mistake such as this, but today the fates require it.

Seeing nothing wrong or wild in Adilakshmi's disheveled state, he asks her, "What do you want?"

"I want Mother."

He leads Adilakshmi into the ashram and the garden where the low white marble tomb of Sri Aurobindo rests beneath the shadow of a tree. As she sits down Aurobindo comes toward her in an extraordinary vision. She sees the trouble he has with his fractured leg, a trouble she knows nothing about that afflicted him in the last years of his life, and he comes forward to embrace and comfort her.

She sits by the tomb for an hour or more, and the visions of Aurobindo continue; Venkat Reddy watches and waits.

"Where is Mother?" she finally looks up and asks him.

He points up toward Sweet Mother's room, which overlooks their garden courtyard, then asks if she wants anything to eat. She does not, so he takes her to his Pondicherry home and there lends her one of his wife's saris.

Mrs. Reddy thinks her a little mad. Adilakshmi understands, for in a similar situation she would think the same herself. The wife is simply separate from the inevitability of the whole process.

For years Adilakshmi has loved the name Nalgonda, a district of Andhra Pradesh that seemed to have no connection with her at all. She is delighted to learn that Venkat comes from there. She is also happy to learn that they both share real devotion for Sai Baba of Shirdi, the saint who has played the role of grandfather in her life. Looking back, they discover many shared reference points in their lives, wandering holy men and men of influence who visited Adilakshmi's family home for its climate and hospitality during the hot summer months and were sought out by Venkat in other times and places. Venkat was also a friend of the husband of Adilakshmi's headmistress, a famous Telugu writer.

For Venkat, the meeting frees him from one of those psychic intuitions of the future that have burned inside him for years. He has long known that somebody would come from a large family of Adilakshmi's caste in Madanapalle to be with him and work with him. When a teacher came to work in the hostel for boys he set up when still a boy himself and he learned the man came from Madanapalle, he kept in his company as much as he could to hear stories of the town.

"I have waited a long time," he says on hearing of Adilakshmi's home.

＝◇＝

MEANWHILE, ADILAKSHMI'S FATHER makes one of his regular devotional trips to the hilltop temple of the god Venkateswara near Tirupati. He has a special relationship with the vast black statue of the god. When some rare event is happening in his family, be it good or bad, the statue shrinks before his eyes to appear small. It does so now, and he hurries home to discover Adilakshmi's absence and her note.

He works his way via the ashram of Ramana Maharshi in the town of Tiruvannamalai to Pondicherry, where a young girl directs him to Venkat's home. He tells his daughter of her mother, who is crying for her return, and tries his utmost to persuade her to return with him, but Adilakshmi is resolved. She is overjoyed to have the suitcase of her belongings he has brought with him, but she will not return to her family life.

Sweet Mother gives Adilakshmi permission to stay in the ashram, and she begins the life of teaching school that will be hers for the next ten years. She writes several letters to the young philosophy professor in the University in Tirupati whom she had hoped to marry. The letters consider the type of life he has chosen for himself and tell him how much happier he could be if he adopted some of the spiritual lessons on life that she is now learning.

◆

THE CONSTANT PRESENCE of Adilakshmi in their household, after her arrival in Pondicherry, taxes Mrs. Reddy's and Jyoti's patience to the limit.

Venkat sees his daughter does not know how to deal with the new woman in his life. He advises her to call Adilakshmi "Aunty."

Jyoti continues to worry about how to relate to this new woman. When her father sits by the ashram's front gate in his post as a receptionist, Adilakshmi sits beside him. When he sits in meditation by the tomb of Aurobindo in the hours before sunrise, Adilakshmi sits on a chair nearby. When he returns after sunset, she is with him again.

"She's always with you," Jyoti complains to her father. "People laugh to themselves when they see her on her chair. While you meditate, she sleeps."

"It's not sleep. It's meditation," her father replies.

"Like this? She meditates like this?" And Jyoti closes her eyes, hangs her head back, and slumps her body askew across a chair. Her lips flutter in a snore.

Adilakshmi and Venkat share a walk beside the ocean. Adilakshmi stands on the beach. Voices from above the waves tell her to take off her gold ring and throw it into the sea. As she prepares to do so, Venkat stops her. He tells her there is no need to obey such instructions. She gives the ring to him instead.

"See," Venkat tells his wife and daughter when he returns home, holding up the ring for their inspection. "Adilakshmi gave me her gold ring."

"What about my property?" his wife retorts, aware that she is being compared unfavorably with this new woman in his life. "I gave you that."

Venkat has always been content with the bland food of the ashram, typically consisting of rice, dhal, and a banana. Now Adilakshmi prepares rich dishes for him, and he learns to savor them.

"Why didn't you do this?" he demands of his wife.

"Give me the money and I will," she retorts.

Jyoti looks back and remembers how Adilakshmi was always happy in those days, always seemed to smile no matter what was said against her. Adilakshmi did not care that her behavior was inappropriate. She did not mind that her constant attendance on Venkat Reddy was misjudged by others, who deemed it shocking that a married man and an unmarried woman should keep each other's company throughout most of their waking hours. Dara, Venkat's friend, comes to Mrs. Reddy and tells her of a vision he has had, in which Venkat is surrounded by all the women with whom he has had affairs. This relationship with Adilakshmi is different from those.

"The women my father went with were always married," Jyoti remembers of this time, "so they maintained some sense of discretion." Adilakshmi didn't care what people thought about her. Venkat was her mentor, so she was happy to spend as much of her waking time with him as possible.

Adilakshmi's dreams and visions are powerful, and she tells

their stories well. Venkat christens her "Savitri" after the Hindu heroine Aurobindo used in his own epic poem.

When Mrs. Reddy's father dies in 1972, Venkat withdraws to the family estate. Adilakshmi keeps to her own Pondicherry apartment and work as a teacher in the ashram. For a while the mother and daughter's life in Pondicherry is untroubled, and their house is their own.

———◇———

VENKAT WRITES LETTERS to Adilakshmi giving news of the girl he has found and telling something of her wonders. The death of Sweet Mother in 1973 deprives Adilakshmi of any sense of the meaning in her life. She receives another letter from Venkat that gives her the strength to carry on with her daily routine. The letter promises that he will bring the girl to Pondicherry for Adilakshmi to meet.

CHAPTER 7

The Growing Girl

After Sweet Mother's death, a wild woman comes to the Aurobindo ashram, one of several who claim to be the new Divine Mother, and positions herself on the same chair that Adilakshmi favored when she accompanied Venkat on his dawn meditations. It is situated beside the stairs that lead up to Sweet Mother's apartment. The authorities decide the chair is jinxed in some way. They remove it and replace it with a potted plant.

Adilakshmi is happy at home in her Pondicherry apartment. Her years of devotion to Sweet Mother have prepared her for a meeting that is to be the sweetest in her life. She has prepared tea. Her old friend Venkat is coming to visit, along with the thirteen-year-old Kamala.

When Adilakshmi recalls this first meeting years later, as she sits in a room in Germany, her face folds itself into a broad smile at that distant time.

"Mother wore red clothes like Durga," she remembers. Durga is a powerful goddess from the Hindu pantheon with a strikingly original and vibrant sense of fashion. "She was so strong and beautiful. 'She's Durga,' I thought, and at the same time she was sweet and lovely."

The words fuel the memory.

"I can see her face still," Adilakshmi says.

———◇———

WHILE THIS TEA PARTY CONTINUES in Adilakshmi's apartment, another tea party is being held some streets away. Its venue is the place that Venkat and Kamala have just left, Venkat's Pondicherry home.

When Venkat's wife heard news from her mother of her husband's obsession with their young servant girl Kamala, there was room for shock but also amusement. At a distance, a servant girl invested with divinity could be funny. Now Venkat has returned from Chandepalle, and he has brought the girl with him. Mrs. Reddy has to deal with the reality of Kamala as her guest.

With her husband and the girl gone for a while, on their visit to Adilakshmi, Mrs. Reddy prepares tea. Then she takes the opportunity to sit down with Jyoti and discuss this latest change in their lives.

Mrs. Reddy and Jyoti are more like two sisters than mother and daughter. They absorb the shocks of Venkat's various passions, of his comings and goings, because the turbulent and changing force that is this man is also a constant in both their lives.

They have each other, they have their faith in Sweet Mother and Aurobindo, and they have the support of the community in the ashram. It is best to maintain their own sense of dignity and not get embroiled in Venkat's life. It is especially hard, however, when Venkat insists on bringing his new female acquaintances into the family home. Adilakshmi was bad enough. Now Venkat is back with Kamala. Though they are not related, Kamala has learned to call Venkat "Uncle." It is a term of affectionate respect as well as convenience.

"If you want to impress your uncle, say you have had visions," Mrs. Reddy tells Kamala when they first meet.

She soon regrets this welcoming joke to Kamala, when she sees how completely it backfires. Kamala takes the advice of the joke to heart and tells ever more powerful accounts of dreams and visions. Her stories hold Venkat entranced.

Venkat is easily enthralled by stories of dreams. Later, when his grandson runs to him and tells him of a vision of Adilakshmi in a tall headdress of gold, golden light streaming all around her, Venkat shouts the news to the rest of the family.

"See!" he proclaims in triumph. "The boy sees Adilakshmi for how she truly is!"

Then everyone laughs, for they know the boy has played a practical joke. Because he has been told that Venkat believes any vision told to him, he made up the story for his grandfather to enjoy. Venkat fell into the young boy's trap. As he sees the boy laugh and hears the family laugh with him, Venkat gets the joke and laughs too.

For years Adilakshmi has been favored by Venkat for the richness of her dreamworld. She soon comes to recognize that she cannot compete with the young girl he has brought to her tea party.

Dressed in red and looking like the goddess Durga, Kamala brings a new sense of purpose to Adilakshmi's life.

<hr />

VENKAT, ADILAKSHMI, AND KAMALA span three generations. Though each was born years apart from the others, they are held together by one common factor in their lives. When they were still in infancy, they each decided that they did not belong to their own

family. They felt convinced that their true family existed in some
divine realm, way beyond the scope of the mess of human drama
they found themselves born into.

This is a quintessential fact of all their lives—they do not belong.

Ironically, this sense of not belonging is a glue that bonds all
three people and holds them together as a unit. Though they belong to no one else, they find they belong to each other.

At Adilakshmi's tea party there is nothing but joy. Venkat,
Kamala, and Adilakshmi are away from their families and have
found each other for the first time. They believe that their shared
destiny has brought them to this moment. Now life must be easier, for they have formed a trinity that brings with it its own perfection. The ways of the world are now immaterial. It would be
foolish to follow society's code, which scoffs at the joy and completeness they find in each other's company.

When Sweet Mother was alive, she formed the center of
Adilakshmi and Venkat's joint life. She was its devotional and
emotional content. Now Kamala has come to them. Adilakshmi is
enchanted by her beauty and brightness and the ancient wisdom
she perceives in the thirteen-year-old girl.

Kamala forms the center of their world. There is no other
world but her.

=◇=

KAMALA RETURNS from Adilakshmi's tea party to Venkat's Pondicherry home, where she dresses up in some of Jyoti's clothes. She
heads out for a walk along the sea front, smart and fashionable in
her puff-sleeved blouse, striding fast along the esplanade between
the ocean and the town. Venkat and Jyoti are some steps behind.

"You're ashamed to walk beside an old man," Venkat calls after
her. Kamala stops to let the father and daughter catch up. Venkat
turns to Jyoti, with words designed for his protégée to hear.

"She thinks she's getting too smart."

Jyoti treats Kamala like her younger sister. She admires her brightness and her speed at learning, and she gives her more of her clothes to wear.

She resents her too. She is angry when Kamala moves into a state of trance, thinking it a sham to impress Venkat. She resents the visions and dreams Kamala recounts to the same degree that Venkat delights in them. She hides things around the house to test Kamala's psychic abilities, then runs the tales to her father when Kamala rises to the bait. She watches how Kamala eats very little during the day, then examines their food store when she wakes in the morning to discover how much food Kamala has come downstairs and eaten in secret during the night.

It is to be expected. A young girl comes into an only child's family and receives the love of the father that was previously the daughter's alone. The title "Divine Mother" is the younger girl's trump card. No matter how much Jyoti may like her and wish to be her friend, she has no match for this claim of supreme divinity. She sees the huge attraction this divine claim has for her father, and so she competes for his love. But since she cannot compete with someone making such a claim of divinity, she seeks instead to deny it.

Kamala, the young Divine Mother, now has an extra existence. She is Kamala, a character in the drama of Jyoti's life. We all have these alternate existences that are born from our relationships with others. Sometimes we merge into them and become the person people take us to be. Sometimes we let ridicule detract from self-belief.

Kamala is not so vulnerable to the opinion of others. She has merged her own self-image so completely with Venkat's expectations of her life, that nothing is likely to shake it.

Many millions of girls are born into the same poor, isolated, rural background she was. This girl who will soon become known as Mother Meera is not simply a phenomenon created by circumstance. She states that she was born with full knowledge of her own divine status and recounts how divine forces set about her subsequent education.

Her upbringing up to the age of eleven offered nothing to deny her perception of her own divinity. There was no school education designed to mold her into the ways of society, no media to invade her thoughts with its opinions and fantasies, no belief system that suggested gods do not roam the earth in human form and play out their dramas above Indian fields. On the contrary, the belief system in her village assured her that such divine play is the natural condition of the world.

Had Mother Meera been born into a country such as Germany, her vocation as a Hindu divine mother would have been sorely challenged. Instead, in village India, it found space to develop within her silence. When she first gave it voice, she spoke to Venkat Reddy, whose life had been lived in longing for tales such as hers. Now Adilakshmi sweeps in, bringing along her own conditioning in the supernatural.

A wider world might seek to deny Kamala's view of herself as a supreme divine being, someone way beyond the limits of humanity. But this is not the world the girl steps into. Her world is the world composed for her by Venkat and Adilakshmi, a circle of assurance, wonder, and belief.

Venkat has given her the only view of herself that matters. Adilakshmi shares that view. Any other is as if seen in a distorting mirror, and Kamala can neither give credence to nor take alarm from such a thing. Kamala knows who she is, a being who spans eternity and the cosmos. She is as interested in matching someone's opinion of her as a land mass is interested in changing its form to concur with the opinion of a sailor out at sea—that is to say, not at all.

Kamala displaces Jyoti in Venkat's life. He does not cease to love his daughter, but the obsessive attention he pays to Kamala sets Jyoti adrift. She no longer has a father she can rely on in any way.

Venkat used to believe that Jyoti was the figure who gave his life meaning. He thought that if he lost her, then he would have no relationship left with the world. When his adoration of Kamala leaves no space in his life for Jyoti, he duly abandons his daughter.

His earlier premonition that this would mean the end of the world for him is now cast as a vision. Instead of being bad news, the loss of his daughter is seen as being something good. It marks the end of his worldly attachments. Kamala is the supreme Divine Mother of the age, and so his love for this new young girl in his life transcends everything that can be found on earth.

He begins to quip, "I have lost the world and found the divine!"

Jyoti watches her father lead Kamala behind the high walls of the Aurobindo ashram and feels the early pain of abandonment.

＝◇＝

IN DEATH, SWEET MOTHER now lies beside Aurobindo in the white marble tomb in the central courtyard of the Aurobindo ashram.

Kamala approaches the tomb for the first time and bows down before it. Kamala is the visitor Sweet Mother has been waiting for, the one who understands the value of her work. Both Sweet Mother and Aurobindo wake up to appear in a vision to the kneeling girl. It is as though the couple are rising from a deep sleep. Aurobindo does not appear as an old man but as a young boy, a companion in age to Kamala, surrounded by his family. Sweet Mother is her elderly self and wanders off to sit beneath a nearby tree. When Kamala rushes to her and climbs onto her lap, Sweet Mother gives the girl a flower. In life she was fond of giving flowers to her devotees, each with a meaning attached to it. The flower she gives to Kamala is white and called "Prosperity."

At this moment, kneeling beside the tomb, Kamala is whisked off on boundless adventures that are recounted in Adilakshmi's book *The Mother*. At first she is befriended by giant snakes, but Aurobindo and Sweet Mother gladly comply with the girl's request

to substitute themselves for the reptiles as her special friends. Together the old couple and the girl journey up between the sun and
moon and stars, then plunge to the depths of the earth's oceans. It
is a swift initiation into secrets of the cosmos, so swift that it happens outside of the bounds of space and time.

The girl who stands up from the tomb has countless visionary
experiences to recount to her mentor, Venkat. A seeming eternity
of tales has been compacted into an instant of her life. During the
six months of this first stay in Pondicherry, she recounts tale after
tale of her cosmic adventures to Venkat.

Venkat asks Jyoti for help in compiling a book of accounts of
Kamala's visions. His preferred title, "Red Roses," is chosen to
echo the title of a book by Sweet Mother, *White Roses*. Jyoti refuses. She reminds him that "red" is a passionate color that would
speak against the spiritual truth of such a book and does not think
a derivative title would be good. The book is never written, although many of Venkat's transcriptions of these stories find their
way into *The Mother*.

The original and perfect audience for these bizarre and exotic
tales is Venkat Reddy, who takes delight in references that extend
the normal bounds of Hindu tales and Aurobindo's and Sweet
Mother's own mystical accounts. For an audience not so re-
hearsed in appreciation, the stories are as mystifying as they are
helpful.

———◇———

IN WRITTEN ANSWERS, Mother Meera assures me that the gods and
goddesses have never become incarnate on earth. Nor am I to
think of them as her brothers and sisters. Furthermore, while
Hindu art gives us images we can assign to these deities, Mother
Meera states that in her own experience these deities do not take
human form.

In *The Mother* Mother Meera speaks of her own appearance
when meeting with someone she presumes to be the Supreme
Mother, called Adishakti.

No one can match my beauty and I have the power to love everything and uplift everything. When I compare myself with Her I find myself more beautiful and more powerful. She does not look beautiful but has everything within Her. What is manifest in me is hidden in Her. When I think of the mystery of this, I am filled with joy.

Mother Meera spends ninety days at the end of 1979 in the company of this Supreme Mother. We might think of Adishakti as being God the Mother, complementary to God the Father, the same force but in its female aspect. After this great divine being ascends, Mother Meera feels herself to be more powerful as a result of their time together, more filled with love. She states that the last trace of fear in her has disappeared.

The account guides us away from seeking similar visionary experiences of our own. There is no need, for the experience Mother Meera had in the visionary realm is now available to us in the physical realm. What is hidden in Adishakti is now available for all to see in the being of Mother Meera.

Although Mother Meera is a beautiful woman, the beauty she speaks about is not to be seen as a beauty of the physical form. It is a beauty that radiates. This is often seen by devotees in the form of light that shines or flares from Mother Meera. It is known to be beauty for the effect that it has upon a person's heart. Someone who does not see the light might be stirred just as strongly by an awareness of beauty when kneeling in front of her body or her image.

Mother Meera speaks of the process of bowing down before the appearance of Adishakti:

When I bowed down I felt I was freeing myself completely and going to higher worlds. I then thought this could happen in the physical world so all humanity can be uplifted and saved by it. May my desire be accomplished quickly.

This is the experience Mother Meera offers to the public in her home in Germany. She embodies the supreme Divine Mother,

and those who bow down before her are doing what she herself
has done in a visionary realm. They enter the process of freeing
themselves from fear, accessing more power and more beauty,
and opening themselves to higher worlds.

In seeing the beauty and the power hidden within Adishakti,
Mother Meera assumes that power and beauty within her own
life. The same can be hoped for by devotees who come to visit
Mother Meera. In the act of seeing the power and beauty within
Mother Meera, they begin to assume the same qualities within
their own lives.

———◇———

MYSTICAL EXPERIENCES TAKE PLACE within the body. They come in
the forms of light and heat. They come as the physical world
shimmers into a fresh view of itself. They come as forces that fill a
body with a sense of boundless space. They come as a body cracks
open to an energy that penetrates it to its very core. They come in
the sensation of being hoisted from the body for the soul-shifting
adventures of dream.

When mystical experience finds expression, it adopts a cultural
form. Mother Meera speaks to Venkat Reddy in their shared language of Telugu, because no other language is comprehensible to
them both. Her tales involve the pantheon of Hindu gods because
these figures are their shared cultural heritage. As Venkat tells
her more of the philosophy of Aurobindo and Sweet Mother, she
identifies the forces at work in her in these new terms.

It is possible to try to shift into the language and culture of
Mother Meera's expression, but to do so is like trying to dream
someone else's dream. Unlike Aurobindo and Sweet Mother,
whose education trained them to express their visionary experiences in terms Western readers might relate to, the visions of
Mother Meera are told as dialogues in which readers are assumed
to already be intimate with her and her culture.

As a child, Mother Meera saw all the gods and goddesses of
her visions simply as lights. As she comes to be able to identify

them by name, their appearance does not alter. They are still divine lights.

As children on the spiritual path, we are free to see divine forces as lights too. There is no need to complicate the matter by attaching names from the Hindu pantheon. Since telling her visions to Venkat Reddy, Mother Meera has made the decision to teach in silence. The inner process that unfolds after meeting her can therefore do so in the language of our own experience.

———◇———

It is too soon for Kamala to be accepted in the ashram as a divine mother. The loss of Sweet Mother is too immediate, and Kamala is too young and inexperienced to be able to reflect back to the ashramites what they wish to see. She is still, very clearly, a young and inexperienced girl, obviously excited by the transition from her village to a more cosmopolitan world. She has the language and social training of village India and finds herself among people who pride themselves on their sophistication.

It is time for Kamala and Venkat to move on.

———◇———

For many of Venkat's friends, the close association between the older man and the young girl seems scandalous, especially since they insist on sharing a bedroom. Although Venkat married his wife when she was only nine years old, that was within the accepted customs of the culture. No matter how chaste and holy the alliance between Venkat and Kamala and that there is an age gap of almost thirty years, the fact that he is still married while traveling with the girl in his care offends people's senses of how human relationships should be conducted. No matter how chaste their relationship might be in reality, outward proprieties were not observed.

Venkat and Kamala visit the aristocratic Nawab family of Hyderabad. This is the family of Venkat's friend Dara. They are one of the principal funders of the Aurobindo ashram, financing the

building of a large official guest house among other contributions. The family assures Venkat that he has found himself "a
jewel" in Kamala.

But neither they nor other friends want the couple to stay for
long.

Venkat knows he needs more time before he can present
Kamala to the world. He decides to use this time to give her a formal education and arranges a place for her in a hostel for or-
phaned girls in the Mygunagore district of Hyderabad. Here she
takes lessons in areas that are seen as vocationally useful, such as
sewing.

She stays at the hostel till she is sixteen, the age when all girls
are required to leave and head out into the world. The hostel experience is not a happy one for her. She is used to education streaming into her consciousness from divine planes and has no interest
in the cramped expectations of the hostel. It is here, though, that
she has one of the fundamental experiences of her life.

She terms this experience the entry of the Paramatman Light.
"Paramatman" is a term for the supreme God. Mother Meera's
declared role is to bring this divine light down into the consciousness of the earth. This light brings with it, as part of its nature, a
knowledge of God. A tree or an animal is more open to its transformative process than are most humans, so her aim is also to
help humanity open to the light.

Kamala's first sight of the Paramatman Light in December
1974 is heralded by ten days of great pain and fear. The voice of
Paramatman roars like thunder in the night, and when the girl
wakes to find herself alone she speaks back to him. The pain she
is going through is too intense. If it continues like this she cannot
live more than a few days. At six o'clock the following morning
she sees the dazzling light of Paramatman for the first time. Two
hours later she wakes up and discovers that her body is well again.
She learns from this experience to associate a certain period of
pain with the onset of the light. She knows to take extra care of

her body, no longer fearing the pain but preparing herself for the light that it heralds.

When her time in the hostel comes to a close, she goes with Venkat back to his village. In a dream the goddess Durga comes to her and announces that the girl Kamala is henceforth to be known as Mother Meera and that she is to wake and pass this instruction on to Venkat Reddy. She duly does so, and she will be known by this name for the rest of her life.

CHAPTER 8

Preparing for the World

The goddess Durga passes a new and important message on to Venkat Reddy through a dream of Mother Meera's. He is not to leave her side for a moment. This is a time of profound change in the sixteen-year-old girl. She sleeps and eats very little and often slips into a state of complete trance for up to fourteen hours a day.

While she is in the trance some villagers come out from the village to sit with her, and as she emerges from the trance state they stand and walk away. It is understood that she needs this period of isolation. It is a time of physical transformation and of learning how to bridge the realms of the spirit and of the earth.

At this time she reports an experience familiar from Aurobindo's descriptions of integral yoga. The top part of her brain seems to open and a steady, unfamiliar flow of force pours in. As long as this force continues to flow, she believes that she can live without food.

Her trances become open-eyed, and gradually she learns to be in a state of continuous trance while performing normal daily activity. Whenever she thinks of people, she sees a clear picture of them, even if they are far away. She finds herself able to continue her cosmic adventures even while she is attending to daily concerns.

Venkat does not try to pursue her education while this process is going on. In *The Mother* he recalls:

> Mother was having so many and such profound experiences, I did not talk philosophy or read the *Gita* to Her or anything. Actually She just wasn't interested. She would cut me short if I started. It is as if all our mental constructions meant nothing to Her. Her education is absolute; She has had Gods and Avatars for Her teachers; She has learnt from a fiery and immediate awareness of the soul and the Supernatural everything she had needed to know.

Arrangements are being made for Venkat to extricate himself from his marital commitments. It becomes unsuitable for the man and the girl to stay on the family land any longer. They drive off to stay for some months with a friend, Sathyanarayana Rao, in the neighboring town of Motkur.

=◇=

OUR CAR PAUSES. The dust settles around us onto the streets of Motkur. The town is in Venkat's home district of Nalgonda in the state of Andhra Pradesh. It stands at a crossroads and lorries thunder between its low buildings. Many in the town make a living from this passing trade. Children press themselves against the walls so the traffic can squeeze by, wipe the dust from their eyes, and walk on.

We have stopped on the edge of town. Pedestrians stop too. A snake is crossing the road. As its head reaches one side, its tail is only just leaving the other. People keep their distance and allow the creature time to pass out of sight and into the grass. Our car moves on, leaving the town and entering the countryside. A young boy in the front seat calls out and the car turns sharply to the right, leaving the road to bounce across a ditch, then up a rutted track into a field.

We are going to visit the boy's father to ask him to travel back in his memory to a time long before his son was born. Now he is retired and his passion is gardening and farming his few acres. He cycles out at dawn and returns to town at dusk, a lifestyle that represents a cherished freedom after his long years as a senior clerk in an office in town. He stands up straight from his digging, his white clothes still fairly free of soil. His hair is gray but thick. He looks out through black spectacles, sometimes directly into people's faces and sometimes at the horizon. He prefers the horizon.

When he was fifteen, he met Venkat Reddy for the first time. Venkat spoke to the boy whenever he made his visit to the post office in town and engaged him in spiritual conversations that whirled the youth out of his regular view of life. He went with the man on a trip to visit Mannikyamma, the holy woman on the hillside. When Venkat moved to the Aurobindo ashram, he went to visit him there.

"I will be forever grateful to Mr. Reddy for taking me from being a normal man to seeing the divine and introducing me to Sri Aurobindo and Sweet Mother," Sathyanarayana Rao remembers.

Venkat visited him several times with the young Kamala. Then he returned when the girl was transformed into Mother Meera. They needed somewhere to stay in the district and chose their friend's house in Motkur.

Their host's devotion is still evident on the white walls of his house's small front room. Portraits of the holy figures in his life hang in their frames: Shirdi Sai Baba, Ramana Maharshi, Sri

Aurobindo and Sweet Mother, and a young Krishna. Each of these figures has the addition of the red spot of Hindu devotion, the kumkum, marked onto the glass to appear on the forehead.

In Motkur, Venkat resumed the young girl's education. In the evening when their host went to sleep he heard them talking, and in the morning when he awoke they were talking still.

———◇———

VENKAT WAS DELIGHTED to have the young girl's company the first time he brought her to Pondicherry. As she sat beside the tomb of Sri Aurobindo and Sweet Mother, he could sense that some spiritual union between the old couple and the young girl was forged. He showed her the ashram and the town, in the way he might have shown a kingdom to a princess who will one day be queen. He felt no sense of misjudgment in his ultimate belief, that this young girl was the divine mother who would continue Sweet Mother's spiritual mission to earth.

However, he also felt some embarrassment during the visit. In his eagerness to install this young teenage girl in her domain, he had failed in his duty to her. The transition from village to city, from the physical sensation of divine powers to their verbal expression, needed much more preparation than he had allowed—especially since that verbal expression had to be subtle enough to meet the probing of the Aurobindo ashram intelligentsia, whose lives had been dedicated to bringing the outreaches of mystical experience down to the level of intellectual understanding.

At first it seemed ironic that he had stayed in the Aurobindo ashram while the young girl of his dreams and his quest was at work in his own village household. In time, though, he comes to see what a blessing it was. Mother Meera will later advise parents not to try to instill formal spiritual practices in their children before the age of twelve, counsel that follows her own experience. During the early period of her life she had the opportunity to simply enjoy the energies that filled her; her education by Venkat came later. In the meantime, Venkat Reddy had what proved to be the last chance to sit and absorb the lessons of Sri Aurobindo's philosophy in the immediate living presence of Sweet Mother, before her death.

The philosophy of Sri Aurobindo provides the structure within which the phenomenon of Mother Meera can grow. It is the intellectual framework that can contain the raw power that Mother Meera transmits. It is the blueprint for their shared public life to come.

Much is made, in the myth that grows around Mother Meera, of her total lack of any education other than that supplied by the gods. No credit is given to this curious, absorbing, and obsessive period of her education, an education into a philosophy of life. Adilakshmi will later add the more basic elements of her schooling such as literacy, but Venkat is her mentor in every skill and stratagem that will contribute to her worldly success.

For these six months in Motkur, day and night for week after week, Venkat prepares his young divine mother to express the truth of her experience according to his understanding of the writings of Sri Aurobindo. Since this is the entire subject of her schooling, it is important to see how the lessons of these months might have shaped her life.

While Aurobindo elaborated the details of his vision with great complexity, its essentials are fairly simple. The universe was created by a God that has both masculine and feminine aspects. The masculine divine is beyond all understanding. The feminine divine manifests itself as the physical universe and as the intelligent power that moves the universe. All created things, whether human being or planet earth, span a spectrum of realities from the lowest (the material) to the highest (pure light and spiritual energy). The entire universe is evolving, as the divine introduces progressively more light into the material world in a way that will lead in the end to its transubstantiation.

Maybe Venkat threw in a story at this point to recapture his young pupil's interest. Perhaps he told her about Sweet Mother's success in reversing the aging process—the older she became, the younger she looked, till in middle age her beauty shone with the radiance of an eighteen-year-old girl's.

In time Sweet Mother tired of this game. Her body wished to age, and she chose to let it. As their physiques deteriorated and death approached, Aurobindo and Sweet Mother internalized their notion of turning the physical world into the divine expression of itself. They decided this ultimate goal of their yoga could be achieved within a single cell of their own bodies. They would focus all their powers on this level, so that this one single cell would be transformed with divinity. Where one cell goes the others will follow, and their bodies duly pass into eternal life.

This is a philosophy for the aging rather than the very young. It is a part of Aurobindo's philosophy Mother Meera will singularly fail to adopt as her own. Perhaps her own truth is saner, or perhaps her youthful concentration wandered whenever Venkat's lessons touched on this subject area.

Aurobindo's story embraces a positive vision of a universe evolving toward ever higher states of consciousness, one in which good in the end triumphs over evil. Unlike most Eastern philosophies, Aurobindo's does not dismiss the material world as an illusion. Instead, he says that the goal of human beings is to keep one foot firmly planted in the material world as they seek to open to the divine.

Aurobindo dismisses all previous forms of religion, spiritual practice, and yoga, both Eastern and Western, as outmoded after his. He tells of his unique experience of the divine and his journey into realms higher than anyone had ever achieved before. In returning, he brought a spiritual energy to earth that he called the Supramental Light. The term "supramental" honors the fact that it comes from a level that surpasses all merely mental efforts to understand it.

Many of the traditional Eastern spiritual traditions state that enlightenment happens when the *kundalini* energy arises from the base of the spine, moves through the system, and finally rises through the crown of the head to merge with the divine. Aurobindo proclaims a new way. He opens a route that reverses this flow of energy, so that we can call the energy of the divine directly down through the crown. The divine then penetrates every part of our being in a progressive way. Through this process the individual becomes enlightened and brings light into the world for the good of others and the world itself, serving as an instrument of divine evolution.

The essential elements that are new in the writings of Aurobindo are these three: the claim that the material universe is evolving toward consciousness as the divine enters more deeply into it; the claim that there is a new spiritual practice of calling the divine light down to penetrate the crown of the head and then the whole body and mind; and the claim that he and Sweet Mother were personally responsible for bringing this special Supramental Light down to the earth for the first time so he could proclaim it to the world.

His philosophy is rare in that it also embraces a complete story of creation from its origin to its goal. It is a tale that captures the imagination of an adult, let alone a child. In its message that all things evolve, including the beings known as avatars who descend directly to earth to promote its well-being, Mother Meera picks up the knowledge that while Aurobindo and Sweet Mother were the greatest divine beings ever to grace the planet, still greater beings will follow them. That is a basic principle of Aurobindo's idea of evolution. She can therefore accept Venkat's assurance that she herself is this new figure of supreme divinity.

Most pleasing to her is the resonance she finds in Aurobindo's story. All the experiences her body collected before meeting Venkat, the encounters with light and heat and spiritual powers, she finds Aurobindo also encountered. The essence of her experience is given voice in her life for the first time in Venkat's stories from Aurobindo. As she wakes to relate a fresh dream or vision to Venkat, she learns how her own story continues the one that Aurobindo left uncompleted.

Mother Meera will grow up to tell a story very similar to Aurobindo's. This story casts her as a character who storms heaven and comes back as the first being to bring down a new, revolutionary light that will cause the rapid evolution of all life on earth. In her case, she will go beyond Aurobindo and Sweet Mother to bring down the highest, strongest, and final light of all, the Paramatman Light, the light of the Godhead itself.

As for the practice, she follows Aurobindo and declares that this light comes down and enters the human from above and that our job is to open to it. The technique she displays at her public gatherings, of holding a person's head and then transmitting light through her gaze, reflects the practice of receiving light that Aurobindo considers one of his central original contributions to spiritual practice.

She has yet to practice this technique. It will come to her when this period of intense schooling is complete and she stages her second coming in Pondicherry.

In order to survive there, one more handicap has to be overcome. Venkat needs funds in order to support them both. During the six months of their stay in Motkur negotiations continue for a marriage settlement. Mrs. Reddy has returned to her home village after her years in the Aurobindo ashram. There is now no possibility of Venkat's harmonious return to his wife and their estate. A deed of renunciation is arranged, whereby Venkat cedes all financial claims on the marriage in return for the funds from the sale of fifty of the estate's two hundred acres. Jyoti objects, for she is pregnant now and recognizes that the deal will disinherit her children. Venkat maintains that the money is a fair return for the work he has put in over the years, and the deal is struck. He receives between thirty and forty thousand rupees.

—◇—

WHAT WAS MOTHER MEERA LIKE at this time?

Sathyanarayana Rao's memory goes back. She was just a girl at first, he recollects. She was pleasant, but there was nothing particular about her. He could not understand the extent of Venkat Reddy's fascination. However, he did notice a marked change in her after her time in the hostel. He attributed this to her first encounter with the Paramatman Light, which Venkat and the girl told him about. She was happy to speak about her own mission to the world now and related it both to him and to others.

"She told me how she had decided to dedicate her life to spread the message of God, to save the world from darkness," he remembers.

She is in touch with him still, writing letters from Germany. He is invited to go and stay with her in Germany, all expenses paid, in return for the kindness and hospitality he once showed to her. He is not inclined to take up the offer, however. He has his personal obligations to his sons and his love of his farm. In Sweet Mother he found the divine relationship he needed, and thanks to Venkat he was able to visit the Aurobindo ashram eight times during her life. The most special occasion of his life was his attendance at the opening by Sweet Mother of the Auroville community, the model for civilization that she established near Pondicherry. His life needs no extra layer of completeness, he says.

If cornered and pressed so hard for a reply that he cannot refuse, is he prepared to swear to the supreme divinity of Mother Meera?

"Mother is in touch with the divine and so she is a divine mother," he declares. "That is as much as I can say."

He is happier talking about Venkat Reddy. That is where his fondness lies. Did Venkat Reddy bring her to consciousness of herself?

"Yes. Mr. Reddy made Mother Meera, and Mr. Reddy made me."

———◇———

WITH THEIR MONEY IN HAND, Venkat and Mother Meera move from Motkur to stay at a friend's house in Hyderabad.

The villagers from her home in Chandepalle are impressed by photographs of Kamala dressed in rich, glamorous clothes, which show how well Kamala is living. Venkat likes to boast to his wife and daughter of the luxuriousness and cost of her new costumes.

"Kamala is wearing a sari worth five or six thousand rupees," he tells them.

A deputation from her home village, including some of Mother Meera's family, travels to Hyderabad and asks her to return on a visit to them before traveling farther. She does so in a vehicle at the head of a small fleet of cars.

She is dressed for the occasion in a beautiful, rich sari. Her hair is loose. It flows thick and wide down her back.

"She looks like Meera," the villagers say when they see her, for Venkat is a good showman and has dressed and groomed his young divine mother for the role she is to play. "Meera. She's Krishna Meera."

Meera was that sixteenth-century poet-saint of India chosen by Mahatma Gandhi as the symbol of India at its time of renewal. A Rajput princess of the same kshatriya caste as Kamala, she was so filled with love for the god Krishna that there was no choice for her but to sing his praises. One of the most striking images of freedom in her poetry is wearing her hair loose.

The role of Krishna Meera is the one Venkat once assigned to Jyoti, the role she refused to play.

Mother Meera sits on her chair on the playground in front of the school building for two or three hours. Everyone in the village steps out to see her. Everyone but Mrs. Reddy. Jyoti has come home to keep her mother company, and the two women lock themselves inside the family home till the party has gone.

The cars drive back through the dusty lanes to the highway, then on to the city of Hyderabad. The return to Pondicherry has been planned, the date chosen with care.

CHAPTER 9

Pondicherry

The French have passion as well as elegance. Passion without elegance is disturbing, like the oceans that heave their water about in fury. Passion with elegance is that particular refinement known as French civilization.

French civilization pauses when it meets the sea. It displays the very best of itself in a fine parade of buildings, neat in symmetry and trimmed with fluted columns, painted white and light blue to share the grace of the skies.

In the south of France the sea is domesticated and called the Mediterranean. The showpiece city is Nice, its trim authority lined up behind a wide boulevard fringed with palm trees.

In India the sea is the Indian Ocean and the city is Pondicherry, but it is nonetheless French for all that. The ocean crashes across sands and smashes on rocks, but when it reaches the land it finds the world very tidy. An esplanade stretches for mile after mile, a wide avenue of emptiness that offers some of the most ordered public space in all of India. Palm trees are planted and thrive in the heat till monsoon winds come, pluck them from their roots, and hurl them over the rooftops. Policemen in their smart blue, buttoned tunics and red peaked caps close the road to rickshaws and cyclists for the occasional motored parade of civic pomp.

At one end of the esplanade the Park Guest House is set to grow as the main accommodation center for visitors to the Aurobindo ashram. Gardeners cut its lawns and tend its flowerbeds and ponds. The seafront promenade from here has an ocean view untarnished by buildings save for one elegant tea room, before reaching the area containing the ashram's ball courts and leisure facilities.

Facing the sea across the esplanade fans swirl in the high ceilings of airy buildings, where civil servants used to glide between shadows on polished floors. While the British had an empire to govern, the French held this patch of India as a showcase for French refinement. As their civil servants withdrew, the Aurobindo ashram moved in to assume control of most of their stately buildings.

There is not much along the fading vanity of this whole seafront, stretching a good way back into the streets of the town, that is not now owned by the ashram in one way or other. The ashram operates guest houses, a cafeteria, shops, printing works, a parade ground, housing units, schools, a swimming pool, a gymnasium, a library, a complex of homes and businesses covering mile after mile, buildings that drop their shade over one another in mutual kindness as the Indian sun flares above.

Sri Aurobindo settled himself into a suite of rooms tucked a few streets in from the weather that hurtles in from the sea. The essence of the ocean floated in through his window, with a flavor that salted his lips, but he did not bother to walk out to meet it. Others might like to stare across water. He preferred the lightscapes of his visions.

Aurobindo and Sweet Mother both now lie in the perpetual shade of the ashram courtyard. It is five years since Sweet Mother's death, and she is sorely missed.

Venkat Reddy has found a house that reflects her life as closely as it can. It is set the same distance in from the sea and just a couple of streets away from the main ashram center.

Mother Meera has been coached for her return to Pondicherry. She has grown, and she has absorbed the inrush of countless forces from divine realms. Now Venkat will do everything in his power to ensure that she is accepted at the heart of her new world. He moves her, Adilakshmi, and himself into a substantial house near the main ashram buildings, 47 Manakula Vinayagar Kovil Street. It is as close to the homes of Aurobindo and Sweet Mother as vacant premises will allow.

———◇———

THE DATE IS FEBRUARY 28, 1978. The monsoon rains have passed and the most severe heats of the summer are still some months away. Venkat, however, had more than climate in mind when he chose this day. The monsoon season might have suited him well. He would have liked lightning to crack and thunder to roar as he brought his young protégée to town. It would have been the voice and power and acclamation of the gods. The particular monsoon-free date was chosen because it is the twenty-second anniversary of the first descent of the Supramental Light.

This anniversary marks an event of supreme importance in the ashram. On this day in 1956 Sweet Mother, with Sri Aurobindo's assistance from beyond the grave, channeled this new light down into the consciousness of the earth as the realization of their joint lifetime's mission. This new, transfiguring divine light promised to propel the earth into its assured evolution from a material into a spiritual dimension.

Now one more light is coming to mark the old light's anniversary celebration.

This light is Mother Meera.

———◇———

NO MATTER HOW BRIGHT a light Venkat brings to the ashramites, it will do little good if they are blind to it. He does his very best to open the eyes of as many as possible.

He starts with his own connections in the Aurobindo ashram, including his former colleague the receptionist at the ashram gates. The gatekeeper remembers his friendship with Venkat Reddy, and when coach parties arrive in the future, each party is directed to pay a visit to Mother Meera in her home around the corner.

There is an eagerness to believe among those in the ashram. They remember Sweet Mother and so have no doubt that life is sweeter when a divine mother is resident among them. Several candidates have appeared over the last few years, most of them marked by an air of craziness. That does not seem to be the case with Mother Meera. The years since her previous visit have carried her out of childhood, and there is a calm about her they find impressive. There is a definite quality about her that invites people to draw closer, to look deeper.

The word is passed around. One by one, people step out from the ashram and approach the house. The fact that the rent for the house is being paid for by the ashram offers some tentative recognition of Mother Meera's status. There is no need to feel disloyal in visiting her.

Gatherings in the house are small. People share Mother Meera's silence and feel some sense of her power. There are question-and-answer sessions at the end of many of the meetings, while pictures of Sri Aurobindo and Sweet Mother hang prominently on the wall.

Mother Meera asks that a picture of Jesus and Mary be found to hang alongside them, aware that there are many in the town who come from a Christian background.

People join an ashram because they do not feel they belong in the world, but loathe the thought of belonging to nothing. An ashram is a reduction of the world to a more manageable scale, where others share your particular streak of madness. It is a hothouse in which a person's spiritual aspiration has a chance to grow into strength, but little thought is given to transplanting this growth back into the climate of the outside world.

Within the hothouse of the Aurobindo ashram, Sweet Mother was the master gardener. She controlled the temperature and trimmed, tucked, and encouraged the growth of her devotees. The fact that many of her private teachings were actually handed out in the form of flowers, the gift of each bloom signifying a spiritual blessing, highlighted her gardening role.

Before her death Sweet Mother commissioned a vast building to be the focal point of Auroville, the community she conceived as a blueprint for the future civilization of the world. The building is a giant sphere composed of glass with a crystal at its center. Devotees and spiritual seekers from all around the globe are encouraged to come here and be recharged by Sweet Mother's divine energy. This is a spiritual hothouse in physical form. Sweet Mother's body lies beside Aurobindo's, the tomb carpeted with infinite care by the day's harvest of flower petals, to form one power point for the ashram. The hothouse at Auroville is another, designed to energize the ashram's evolution after the holy couple's death.

Ashramites are an exotic species. They might well wither in the outside world, but in their carefully maintained microclimate they can know themselves as creatures of rare beauty. As individuals they contain little balance between the ways of the world and the ways of the spirit, but as a collective they feel their ashram is doing the world some good. The material rampaging of the outer world finds some balance in the strength of their own spiritual ambitions. This is similar to the "trickle-down effect" promised by right-wing politicians, that the wealthy become so very rich they can afford to take care of the poor.

The ashramites seek spiritual wealth. They excuse any impression of selfishness with the knowledge that what they have can be passed on to those less fortunate than themselves. Accordingly they chase vision after vision, an upward journey through realms of light.

It seems like the bravest journey imaginable. However, the very fact that they choose to perform it in an ashram is a sign of their dependence rather than their independence. They appreciate the holy spirit of Sweet Mother and Aurobindo that pervades their atmosphere, but would welcome some of the more immediate advice Sweet Mother used to offer.

They know the dangers of the ego on their chosen path, and they are aware how easy it is to be held in the spell of fantasies or hostile forces. They need confirmation that what they are doing is good and that they are on the right track. Sweet Mother had the authority to reassure them and sometimes correct them. Now that she is gone, they have a need for a replacement, someone who is far enough ahead of them on the path to give them appropriate counsel.

It is possible that Mother Meera is this figure. That is the role they wish her to play. They bring their stories and their questions to her. They tell her accounts of their highest mystical experiences.

"Is this so?" they ask when each story is complete. It takes daring to reveal something so intimate, to recount their visionary experiences in such depth. These stories are the most tender parts of their lives, their reason for living. Ashramites are primed for the world to treat their most sacred experiences as nothing, degrade them with the label of fantasies. They look for Mother Meera's confirmation that what they have achieved is no fantasy at all, that it is real, that it is so.

"Is it so?" they ask.

"Yes," Mother Meera responds.

The relief is immense. Their lives are given ultimate worth by the comment.

But Mother Meera has not yet finished. Compared to Sweet Mother's, her comments are extraordinarily succinct, yet they are telling.

"But it is nothing," she adds.

And this is all she adds. Somewhat like the oracle at Delphi, Mother Meera tends to stop before her statements have any real substance. They point toward a lesson, but stop short of real elucidation. The oracle offers a riddle rather than guidance. People take its message and hurtle through life until they have discovered the oracle's wisdom for themselves, often after learning from their mistakes.

What wisdom can we take from this brief sentence? One interpretation accords with statements Mother Meera will make in the future. A vision is nothing until its lesson is learned, until it is brought back into the play of a person's life. A vision that leads on to another vision is simply a further means of escape. We must stop, allow a vision to work its full magic within our being, stick with it through the years till we have taken a firm hold on its lesson, and let it open our perception of our changing world and the part that we play in that process of change.

Mother Meera has moved out of any sense of belonging to the world. She is her own force and has established her own conventions. The ashramites have not. They have joined an ashram in order to have a sense of belonging. Because they see themselves in relation to others rather than dare to hold a mirror to their own actions, they are still in the realm of competition. One individual tries to do better than another. They know that what happens to one person happens to all, but still retain their individual identities rather than see themselves conjoined to every other facet of creation.

"Your visionary experience is so. But it is nothing."

They hear this and think Mother Meera is saying, "It is nothing compared to mine, compared to all that I have achieved."

They are still in the stage of passing judgments on the world and therefore judge Mother Meera to be arrogant. They may well be right. Certainly the promotion of Mother Meera sets her in competition with the memory of Sweet Mother.

Yet to stop at the level of judgment is to refuse to complete the process of our inner work. "Your visionary experience is so. But it is nothing . . . until you work with it, fashion it into the fabric of your life in the world."

That alternate reading of Mother Meera's comment is a good lesson, even if it is not the one that the ashramites wish to hear.

Venkat Reddy notices that those who come from the ashram bring puffed-up hopes along to Mother Meera. He sees that they leave with those hopes deflated, which does his ambitions no good at all.

He begins to ask visitors whether they speak Telugu. If they answer that they do not, he tells them how Mother Meera only speaks Telugu and so cannot talk with them. If they can speak Telugu, he tells them that this is a period in which Mother Meera is keeping silent. While he still cherishes every word she says to him, he begins to see the value of public silence. Sweet Mother was famous for her scheduled question-and-answer sessions. Her responses delighted devotees with the lucidity of their expression, the depth of their learning, their fulsomeness, their insight. Since Venkat is hoping people will make a direct association between Sweet Mother and Mother Meera, he sees that it is wrong to make too much of a display of Mother Meera's powers of discussion. Astute though she may be, her discourses do not stand up in comparison with Sweet Mother's.

"She talked too much," Mother Meera will later remark about her predecessor.

Mother Meera's power is in her presence and in the light she transmits. A principal strength in her teachings is her insistence that people take whatever they receive from her and test it within their regular lives. She preaches against withdrawal in contemplation of God, since this encourages the vanity of people's perceptions. God is everywhere, in everything we do, so we must let that consciousness of God flow into our daily actions.

For now, Venkat encourages a stronger display of her silence.

All his coaching in Motkur, when he spoke to Mother Meera of Aurobindo's philosophy for hour after hour, will still be put to the test, however.

Mother Meera is troubled by the periods of ill health that have dogged her since birth, the fevers and pains and headaches. She explains this to someone in the ashram by saying she is so busy with her work on higher planes that she neglects to take the necessary care of her health.

The ashram doctor, Dr. Bhose, is called in to examine her. Sensing the return of an embodied divine mother to the community, he is so impressed by the qualities of the young woman that he calls together leading figures of the ashram to meet her.

The meeting takes place in the library at the home of his friend, Dr. Arabinda Basu. Along with the host and Dr. Bhose, the ashramites Amal Kiran and Nirodbaran form what becomes something of an interviewing panel, with a list of prepared questions.

Dr. Bhose has since died. Three men, astonishingly considering their tremendous age, remain.

═══◇═══

"I ASKED AUROBINDO for only three things," Nirodbaran remembers. "One was . . . I have forgotten, but the others were to keep my hair and not get a paunch."

The request has worked. His hair is black and fairly thick, his figure is lean. His hearing has failed a little—perhaps the reason that the voice of Aurobindo shouts when it comes to wake him at two o'clock every morning, years after the master's death. His own voice is loud and clear. He is dressed in a singlet and sky-blue dhoti. His walk is steady, his handshake firm, his whole bearing abnormally strong for a man of ninety-two.

Nirodbaran became the close companion of Sri Aurobindo during the last twelve years of Aurobindo's life. The fractured leg Aurobindo sustained in a fall left him in need of some help. Nirodbaran took on the role of receiving dictation of the poem *Savitri*, which grew to become the longest epic poem in the English language.

Water boils for tea on a brazier at the back of the wood-paneled room that is his home. The walls are filled with photographs of Sweet Mother and Aurobindo. The portraits of Aurobindo, with his straggly beard, long white hair, sharp nose, and fearsome expression, show the archetype of Merlin, while the pictures of Sweet Mother's face are dominated by the hawklike intensity of her eyes, which one could imagine never blinking. The couple now lie in their tomb only yards away, for the door of Nirodbaran's quarters opens onto the central ashram courtyard.

Mother Meera herself once came here for tea. Nirodbaran's young niece sat opposite her, enjoying the silence, gazing into the astonishing depths of Mother Meera's eyes.

Nirodbaran recalls the more formal meeting with Mother Meera, when he was one of the delegation sent to quiz her in the library of his friend Arabinda Basu. He remembers some difficulty with the nature of the translation as handled by Adilakshmi. The full purport of questions and answers did not get through. However, there was truth in what he heard that day. There was something genuine, there was some power there.

He is satisfied with his own divine mother, however. He needs no other, even though the ashram is not the same since her death.

"Aurobindo and Sweet Mother are one. They became incarnate in two bodies because that was necessary to do the work.

Mother was creative. She says this herself. Aurobindo brought down the force, brought down the light, and Mother applied it. She was always with us with great energy. Aurobindo was aloof.

"In the ashram we do the same things, run the school in the same way, keep to the same rules, but now there is less vigor. Sweet Mother had enormous vigor, enormous energy. Now she puts us to the test."

Nirodbaran often joins the seniors for their exercise routine on the parade ground. Ancient men and women in their blue and white gym clothes march up and down in the dust, the frailer ones occasionally slipping out of rank to recover, while their instructor barks instructions at them. Then everyone sits down to listen to a recorded speech from Sweet Mother, a piece of her French conversation conjured up from former years and amplified beneath the stars.

It is all very valiant and a little sad.

———◇———

AMAL KIRAN SHIFTS HIS WHEELCHAIR about with agility, moving between his typewriters, desks, and bookcases. His speech consists of sentences formed with exquisite linguistic precision, the spearhead of a fierce intellect.

He was in his late seventies, deep into a spiritual odyssey that brought him into close contact with two great masters, when he joined the party to interview the seventeen-year-old Mother Meera. The gulf in age was great, and when he fired out his questions he grew impatient that they were weakened through the medium of translation into and out of Telugu.

Mother Meera was a simple, gentle girl, he remembers. From looking into her eyes she seemed a good person to know. Her experiences as she related them could have been on the vital plane rather than a higher one, and she was not able to give some of the more complicated answers. However, on meeting her later he sensed that she was indeed open to higher realms.

Amal Kiran looks at least as ancient as his age—ninety-one. Convex discs are set into the centers of his thick glasses to magnify his vision. He glares through them when offering his harshest comment. "Claims that Mother Meera is bringing down a light beyond Sweet Mother's are fanciful," he declares.

Sweet Mother is the ultimate fact in his life. The main characteristic he recalls is her tolerance, especially her tolerance of the "complex and distorted man" that he himself is. It makes no difference how many times you fall; it is your efforts to pick yourself up again that matter.

Aurobindo's is a very hard yoga, its ultimate aim being the divine transformation of the physical body. Amal Kiran believes that this can ultimately be achieved, so that there is no need for mortality, and that it can be achieved by one person as a model for all on earth. He thinks that with the deaths of Aurobindo and Sweet Mother this physical transformation for humankind, something he calls "the Supramental transformation," was rendered impossible in a complete form for now.

In extreme old age, he is an example of a man whose life is guided by the presence of a divine mother within his heart. His aim is to move farther into the light of Aurobindo and Sweet Mother, to go higher, wider, and deeper, and to maintain within himself an inner poise and equilibrium. Sweet Mother is dead. He recognizes the loss of such a being in a physical form, but has no need of a replacement. She rests in his heart, and when his heart finally stops beating, he will find her there.

———◇———

MOTHER MEERA ENTERS Arabinda Basu's house through its garden and turns right into the large front room that forms the library. The high shelves of books do not dull the sense of light that fills the room. She settles herself on a chair and prepares to meet the four grand old men who form the unofficial council from the Aurobindo ashram.

The ashram stands for the world at this point. This is the most noteworthy arena into which Venkat can introduce Mother Meera. If she can pass official scrutiny here, she proves able to manage herself on a wider public stage.

Mother Meera has had her schooling during the months in Motkur. Venkat has prepared her for the types of minds she is about to meet. From Venkat's stories she knows more about the philosophy of Aurobindo than is obvious in her shy demeanor. Much depends on the outcome of this meeting. She faces the prospect of either ridicule or approval.

Venkat is nervous. Adilakshmi is nervous too. They have both lived lives that are not significant within the ashram's hierarchy and are now in an official meeting with those who form the very top strata. Their hopes depend on a young girl who is fairly fresh from Indian village life and who can only speak in Telugu, a language foreign to these august gentlemen.

The young Mother Meera sits with her hands folded on her lap and appears to be quite calm. She waits patiently for the inquisition to begin.

Adilakshmi translates. The men of the council feel that their questions are depleted by her abilities as a translator. They sense that Mother Meera also lacks sufficient vocabulary in her own language to understand the philosophical concepts they introduce into their conversation. They study her and decide that they are meeting a very simple girl.

Her answers impress them, however. One answer is particularly striking.

They ask about the *kundalini*, the serpentlike force that lies coiled and dormant at the base of the spine. Most Hindu traditions see the awakening of this force as a vital step toward enlightenment. The ashramites ask Mother Meera how we can best draw up this power from within ourselves.

It is a trick question. Most Hindu pundits of any training would have a ready answer of some sort. It is the belief of the ashramites, who have studied the integral yoga of Aurobindo, that a new power of transformation is now at work in the world. If Mother Meera is truly continuing the work of Aurobindo and Sweet Mother, she should know this.

Mother Meera's answer is immediate, direct, and simple.

"It is better to invoke the power from above," she tells them.

The answer impresses them, because it accords with their own vision of the truth. Since the girl very obviously has no education and since they know nothing of Venkat's coaching and hold him in scant respect in any case, her answer must have come from personal insight.

The four men share their impressions when Mother Meera, Venkat, and Adilakshmi leave them alone together. They worry for the girl. Her answers appear to have come from somewhere beyond her education, to stem from a depth of great personal experience. They feel able to pass on the news that they have seen nothing to discredit the claim that she is a divine mother and that they have heard things suggesting the claim might possibly be true.

However, the girl is still young. While they see the potential within her, they feel her essence rests in her simplicity. They share their concerns that she will be overpromoted, that in the act of bringing her to the world's attention Venkat will drive her beyond her natural abilities. They fear that what they see as purity in her might be spoiled. She is already something wonderful. If she is sold to the world in terms that are not her own, her fine simplicity might be lost.

———◇———

IN HIS SEVENTIES, Arabinda Basu looks back across the twenty-five years to the time of the meeting. Something of a stern figure when away from home, back within the walls of his library he lets the boy within himself shine through. His hair hangs in soft, thick, gray waves and he blinks through his gold-framed spectacles, thinking his way back and coming upon fondness.

Mother Meera made a happy impression on him. She returned to his house alone some time after the meeting with the council. He remembers her calmness and the great depth to her eyes. He recalls the transformation in the girl after her visionary experience when kneeling before Aurobindo and Sweet Mother's tomb. He remembers seeing "good beyond the normal goodness."

He steps outdoors, holds his hands in the *namaste* of Indian blessing, and sends his regards to Mother Meera and Adilakshmi in the life they have fashioned for themselves in faraway Germany.

⸺◇⸺

A DOCUMENT containing a transcription of the council's meeting with the young divine mother passes from hand to hand around the ashram. A ripple of excitement gathers into a wave.

Some regard the old men of the council as foolish for being taken in by Mother Meera. Ashrams suffer from politics the same way institutions in the outer world do, and those who are in positions of authority will always have their critics and opponents.

Others are thrilled to hear the positive outcome of the meeting between the elders and the girl. Many ashramites are ready to accept a new divine mother among them. However, they are not ready to have Mother Meera pushed on them as the supreme Divine Mother. The power they find in Mother Meera is soured by the effects of Venkat's presentation of her, and the ashramites keep away. Of the many hundreds who go to visit her, only one member of the ashram, an American woman, stays the course and dares to think of herself as one of Mother Meera's devotees.

After the meeting with the council from the ashram, a journalist from U.N.I., a government news service, visits the library where the meeting was held to interview Arabinda Basu. The subsequent article announces the arrival of a new divine mother in Pondicherry. Mailbags of response arrive from all over India with questions about Mother Meera's role and identity and requests for help.

===◇===

MANY OF THOSE who now come to see her are foreigners, attracted to the Aurobindo ashram but not enough to become members. One, a young Canadian from Quebec called Jean-Marc, is the first to receive Mother Meera's unique form of blessing. He kneels before her and she takes his head in her hands; then he sits up and they look into each other's eyes. This pattern of blessing comes naturally to her.

A new name for Mother Meera occurs to Jean-Marc at this first meeting—"Eternal Mother." For the half hour he is with her he repeats the name over and over. Each day for the following months he returns, often bringing friends, experiencing the most transformative and happy period of his life.

===◇===

IN THE SUMMER OF 1978, a few months after Mother Meera's arrival in Pondicherry, her title "Divine Mother" takes on a new meaning. A child is born somewhere in the Western world. It is a baby girl, born into a family of substantial means.

In some ineffable way, Mother Meera sees herself as being the mother of this baby. She gives her the name Loka Shanti Shakti, meaning "The Mother of World Peace." Mother Meera will later intimate to devotees that she and this young girl will meet just once or twice in their physical lives, but for now it is unclear whether the baby will live long.

Loka Shanti Shakti's work begins when she is two months old. This early start saves her from being tarnished by human consciousness. The foundation of world peace is a considerable task for a young baby, and there are fears that she will not have the stamina to both do her divine work and live. Mother Meera chooses to share the burden.

The work taxes both mother and daughter. On April 2, 1979, when the baby is eight months old, devotees learn of her existence for the first time. It is wondrous news, but causes great concern among them, for no sooner do they hear of this baby than they learn she is unwell. There is distress, and there are prayers for the baby's well-being.

The prayers seem to take effect. On the following day, Mother Meera announces that her "mystic child" is better and states something of their joint mission.

Loka Shanti Shakti makes a brief appearance in Adilakshmi's *Mother Meera*, before the information is edited out of the official myth in the book's later editions, which appear under the new title of *The Mother*. Mother Meera declares:

> There are three steps in the work of the Mother. I, Mother Meera, am helping people to surrender themselves to the Divine and to the Light, which has to come first otherwise nothing will be possible. Loka Shanti Shakti is working for peace. When that is established, Sri Aurobindo and Sweet Mother can effect the transformation. Of course I am doing many other kinds of work too. I am helping everyone who needs me.

In Germany in future years Venkat will take delight in telling devotees about this infant divine mother. His belief in an ascendancy of divine beings stems from his understanding of Aurobindo's philosophy. He learned from his readings that nothing is static, that evolution takes place in every aspect of creation. Divine beings and incarnations of God on earth are as much part of creation as anything else and must therefore duly evolve. The divine beings who are born later in history are therefore greater than those who were born earlier.

He is consistent in his belief. His sense that Mother Meera has inherited the powers of Aurobindo and Sweet Mother and adds qualities of her own to surpass them, even while the forces that are Aurobindo and Sweet Mother are still at work after their deaths, does not endear him to devotees of that couple. However, as Mother Meera surpasses all who went before, so, he will later tell devotees, Loka Shanti Shakti will surpass even her.

———◇———

THIS PRIVATE COSMIC WORLD of Mother Meera goes through an explosively rich period during the first year of this stay in Pondicherry. Back on her first visit to Aurobindo and Sweet Mother's tomb, they rose from their graves and adopted her into their care. She has related many stories of their mythic adventures together.

Now she announces a stage in the spiritual transformation of the world that is unique to her own incarnation, reported in *The Mother:*

> On July 9, 1978, light entered into my body through my finger-nails, like a procession of ants. It was an indescribable white, blue, red, and golden light, a mixture of all these colors. I saw the light pass physically through my fingers. In my eyes I noticed light like the rays of the sun, which created a strange movement in them. When the light entered my body it was shaken as if by an earth-quake. My sense organs were cut off and I could neither see nor hear. The light entered every cell. The cells were everywhere jangled by light, moving and changing in it. I felt the whole process as one of complete cleansing.
>
> It was impossible to control my body. My mind, my heart also became helpless. I felt as if I had no bones or nerves and felt my heart going weaker. I could not pick up any objects; they just fell out of my hands. I could not walk and felt as if my knees and not my feet were standing on the floor. My body was as weak and supple as a snake and couldn't stand upright.

We are told that this bringing down of divine light is the central mission of Mother Meera's time on earth. It is not a matter of bring-ing this light into existence, but bringing it into usage. Electricity was around in the Dark Ages, but no one knew of its existence, let alone how to harness and apply it. This "light" has always been there, but now Mother Meera is applying it to creation.

And not just to creation on earth, Adilakshmi reminds me. "Mother brings light to the whole universe."

Animals and plants take it in more easily than humans, but we can be aware of it and open to it more freely than we do. On November 21, 1978, Mother Meera reports how the Supramental Light directed by Sri Aurobindo and Sweet Mother powered into the earth with force for one minute. The earth then set about the process of absorbing this brief, sustained transmission.

She also describes the physical effect this light might have on some people whenever it comes:

> It enters from above the head, through the fingernails or through the soles of the feet. Wherever it enters, it produces a burning sensation and that part of the body feels numbness. If the body is not strong physically, severe pain is felt for ten to fifteen minutes, as severe as a scorpion sting. Those who are unwilling or unreceptive feel the pain especially. When the body is fully charged with light, even though the pain is severe it should not reject the light. On the contrary, aspiration for it must grow, despite its effects. The pain may last for ten or fifteen minutes but will vanish completely after two hours. Afterward a supreme Joy and Peace will be felt and all obstacles to the furthest spiritual progress will be removed. You will know that you have received the light because you will experience love of all humanity and an infinite concern for all life. You will be able to work and save the world and at the same time feel a complete and peaceful detachment from the world.

On the January 2, 1979, Mother Meera tells Venkat how she has joined forces with a whole host of gods, goddesses, and holy beings to pray for a new light, termed the Paramatman Light because it is sent directly from God. This is the light she first encountered in her own body during her years in the girls' hostel in Hyderabad. Now she is determined that it should power into the earth in the same way that it powered into her body—for unlike Aurobindo and Sweet Mother she does not see the transformation of the earth and of her own body as being the same thing.

Without color but of a dazzling brightness, this Paramatman Light fills every cell of creation. Instead of pain, it fills a body with ecstasy.

"In all things everywhere, in all beings, the Light is hidden, and it must be revealed," Mother Meera declares in a written statement issued in Pondicherry. "If we try with all our hearts, we will be successful. I want the Paramatman Light to blossom everywhere."

<hr>

BEYOND THE CALM of the seafront and the area dominated by the Aurobindo ashram, Pondicherry stretches back into the chaos and noise and business of the average Indian city. The buildings run for miles till they taper off in a series of rattan shacks on either side of a narrow earthen road.

Fat or thin, ugly or beautiful, cackling or silent, wild or demure, divine mothers are offered to us in many forms. It is hard to disassociate an energy from its means of transmission. This brief pilgrimage away from the town helps us experience something of the divine feminine essence unattached to a human form.

Near the hamlet of Veldrampet is the beginning of a narrow track raised as a divide between dry paddy fields. In December when these fields flood and pilgrims walk along the track, it appears as if they are walking on water.

A yellow illuminated sign hangs on an open building so that it looks somewhat like a shop. In Tamil it announces that this is the Sri Durganandamma Temple.

This is the oldest temple in the district, dating back four hundred years or so. Water is drawn up by bucket from a deep well, so that hands, feet, and face may be washed before approaching. There is no front wall, for this building is essentially an altar and worshipers sit on the bare earth in front of it. There are rattan walls and a thatched roof, to provide shelter for the head of the goddess, which stands at the top of a row of stone steps. Made of black stone, the head sits directly on the platform. Her hat rises like a cone ringed with layers of berries, and all around her is a stone garland of fire.

Unlike most temples in India, which are served by male Brahmin priests, this temple to the goddess is attended by a woman. She is a fine stout young woman with bright eyes and a merry face, her body bound tightly in a bright green sari. With camphor and incense she conducts a ceremony before the small Ganesh in his own miniature shrine at the front of the steps, the elephant god appearing as happy as ever to be dancing in attendance. The camphor is then set aflame before the goddess Durga herself.

Durga's stone shrine is at the head of the temple. It is tempting to stand fixated in front of this shrine made by human hands and presume the temple consists simply of this. This is the way we live, after all. We are so focused on the products of humanity that we fail to see how everything human is placed within the boundless and magnificent scale of all of creation.

This shrine can also, however, alert us to the temple that surrounds it. Human creation can do that; it can form a jump-off point into the divine. We are locked in a narrow perspective, interested in the world as a reflection of ourselves. But we can change that stance and see ourselves and our achievements as a reflection of the world.

Here in this temple we can practice this. The temple is large, but it has no ceiling made by humans, no walls of human construction. The temple's body is outlined by two lines of mighty palm trees unlike any others in the district. Their trunks have a girth of around ten feet. With their broad fronds on top, they look like cosmic pineapples. They define the shape of this temple without constricting it at all. In the space between them the walls open out on horizons of more trees, fields, and distant blue sky.

The palm fronds fringe the edge of the ceiling, which is also composed of sky. Sometimes blue, sometimes white, sometimes black, sometimes blazing with sun or spangled with stars, it takes on all the colorings of our outlook on the cosmos.

Beneath this ceiling is the temple floor. It is composed of grass. The foundations of this grass are our entire planet earth. There is no longer any need to puzzle over why the goddess in the stone shrine is only represented by her head. The head pokes through the crust of the earth, topped by her crown of flames, so she can breathe creation into the air. Her body is actually formed of the planet earth itself.

Within this monument to the goddess Durga, seated on the green temple floor, we can know ourselves to be deep inside the goddess herself. Her touch not only surrounds us, it fills us, and yet it does more than that too—it composes us. Her descent around and through the body is a gentle wash of peace. We can know that we are energy and not simply matter and that this touch of the goddess is her eternal work. It is not simply a touch but our very composition. We are composed by God in every instant of our being.

This temple in the countryside of Pondicherry is a metaphor for the nature of the world. Through the open walls of palm trees, beneath its living floor, throughout the sky that lights and darkens as its roof, and consisting as the atoms of our very own being, God is living as her own creation.

———◇———

CREATION IS TIMELESS and ubiquitous, yet it is also here and now. The cosmos is expanding, but as an image of itself. It is similar to a seed, which contains within itself its whole history as a tree, its ultimate growth through each of its seasons, and its eventual decay back into the ground. It is consigned to a process of constant change within the image of itself.

In some of her Hindu aspects, the divine feminine force can seem demonic. Death is a vital part of the creative flow, sweeping aside the old and making way for the new, and Hindu goddesses are empowered with every quality of destruction.

Mother Meera lays claim to all these forces of the divine feminine, but the Hindu aspect she most favors is that of the goddess Durga. This goddess holds love as a greater part of her being than do other forms of the goddess. She is imbued with a magnificent degree of patience.

Images of Durga hang on the walls of Mother Meera's German and Indian homes. Most pictures of Durga show her with a sword raised in the air, but the ones in Mother Meera's homes are chosen because they are different from the norm. They show Durga with her sword thrust into the ground.

What is transmitted through Durga's sword, which she thrusts into the earth and so into the substance of ourselves?

It is light, and it is also consciousness. If we can perceive the process of constant and perpetual change, in which everything throughout the universe is rendered radically and totally new with every moment, because it is essentially a flow of one energy in and out of matter through its many forms, we can then bring consciousness to this process of change.

Goldfish breathe, flowers bud, knowledge bounces off satellites and appears on screens, people fall in love, winds sigh, rains fall—our world is composed of nothing but a constant stream of interlaced miracles. When we grow numb to it, consciousness reawakens us to wonder.

Consciousness is one more miracle through which more miracles can flow.

Out of India

Until the age of forty-one, shortly before his first meeting with the young Mother Meera, Venkat Reddy is in fine health. Then he takes on a mission that breaks him.

A Sikh friend of his great friend at the Aurobindo ashram, Dara, is sentenced to death for murder. Venkat is petitioned to help gain his reprieve. He takes the commission as far as the president of India in New Delhi, and the reprieve is granted.

While Venkat is staying with the family of the condemned man, however, a man appears to him in a vision. Venkat describes this character to those in the house. They are silent a while, in obvious shock, and then tell him that he has given them the description of the murdered man. This man tells Venkat to stop his efforts, for the man arraigned for murder is indeed guilty.

Venkat returns from New Delhi, bringing back the reprieve but also a fever.

"This is not your sickness," Dara's brother tells him.

Some people speculate that Venkat's subsequent chronicle of ill health is the dead man's curse. It may indeed have been that the extreme efforts he undertook to help out in the case were too much for his health. Whether the two facts are linked or not, Venkat was noted for excellent health before this time and illness afterward.

Venkat spends occasional periods in the hospital. His body may be weak, but his will persists. He is given a bed next to a man who curses and blasphemes continually. Venkat pleads with him to stop, and when this does not happen, he vows that he will not look the man in the face until the cursing ceases. While his back is so turned in the night, the man dies and is carried away.

In 1972 his daughter, Jyoti, has a dream in which Venkat is dying. A bubble is rising out of him and floating away and she knows it is his soul. In the dream, which she credits as an experience as real as anything in her waking life, she speaks with Sweet Mother.

"Please save him," she pleads.

"He's dead. I can't," Sweet Mother replies.

"Savitri brought someone back from death," Jyoti replies, invoking the story of the Hindu heroine whose life Aurobindo told in his epic poem.

"Okay," Sweet Mother replies. "But he must do yoga."

Her father is suffering from TB at the time and has a very high blood-sugar level. Jyoti tells him her dream.

Another time she worries about his illness and prays to Sweet Mother to relieve him of any suffering. Instantly she feels a great pain in her own chest. It is so severe that she fears for her own life and asks Sweet Mother to stop. She recovers.

She shares this experience with her father too, who admits that yes, there was some relief for a while that coincided with her request and subsequent pain.

The early years of Mother Meera, from the age of eleven when she first articulates her sense of divine mission until her arrival in Germany less than ten years later, must all be seen from within the context of Venkat's poor health. All his life he has been on a quest to find her. When he does so, he is forty-six and already fading fast.

For Venkat, the difference in their ages is not so much shocking as absurd and sad. For years he has had as much stamina as any man alive. Now it is fading when he needs it most. He and Kamala could have made a strikingly beautiful couple. Now the world will only see them as an old man and a girl. He knows that this young child needs time to grow into her public role, and for five years he grants her the space in which to grow. Yet he also knows his own time is limited. She has her role in life to fulfill, but so does he. If he is to promote her effectively, he must use every available moment of health, make every possible marketing move, raise every available rupee, tap every known connection. He found the young girl in his Indian village and proceeded to give her his India.

She arrives in Pondicherry in February 1978. She will take her first plane flight to the West in September 1979, at the invitation of Canadian devotees. The time allowed Venkat to move Mother Meera from village India to the world stage, from her seat in the school playground at Chandepalle to an auditorium in the city of Montreal, is less than two years.

As the marketing manager for the enterprise that will grow into the worldwide phenomenon of Mother Meera, Venkat can justify using every ploy in the book, because he has ultimate faith in his project. He knows there is a purity to the divine force that is Mother Meera, the force that both she and he ultimately serve. He trusts there is a truth to the experience of her presence that nothing will be able to tarnish.

This is the principal danger for those who proclaim themselves to be God on earth. There is no one to answer to beyond oneself.

When you think of yourself as God, your own needs are quite simply the ultimate good. Whatever means you use to meet those needs are therefore justifiable, whether the world praises them as good or condemns them as wicked.

Venkat reckons the world cannot know the good that is Mother Meera until it comes to see her. It won't be changed until it is confronted by her power. And so he must speak to the world in terms that the world will understand, in terms of power and beauty and the personal benefits of the kind of transformation he has on offer.

He will live long enough to look at his failed efforts in the Aurobindo ashram in Pondicherry and speak of them as one of his favorite jokes.

"How could I expect them to believe me?" he asks. "I had already brought my young wife to them, saying she was the Divine Mother! If I admit I was wrong then, why should they believe I am right now?"

—◇—

AT FIRST THERE SEEMS TO BE every chance of establishing Mother Meera in the Aurobindo ashram. But the longer they stay there, the more forlorn Venkat sees this hope to be. Many ashramites come and pay a visit or two and are never seen again. The excited buzz of conversation that greeted her second stay in Pondicherry is now touched with words of scorn.

The ashramites belong to an institution. They come to Mother Meera with a set of expectations. It is a prescriptive rather than an open approach, and she has no desire to trim the breadth of her powers into the confines of their expectations.

Those who come from overseas, already broken from much of their conditioning by the culture shock they undergo in India, are steadier in their steps toward devotion. Whatever Mother Meera is, she is slightly beyond their ill-defined expectations. They keep on coming.

———◇———

FRANK, A FRENCHMAN who has made his home in Germany, meets Mother Meera in 1978 and sends a letter from Pondicherry to his friends back home.

"The Mother is alive," he writes.

"Oh, well," the friends say to themselves. "If that's what Frank thinks, that's okay."

They are used to similar slogans. "Jesus lives," people say, because they feel his touch within their heart.

Frank returns. The friends find him changed. Some power radiates about him. Selling their belongings to fund their journey, three of them buy tickets to accompany him back to Pondicherry.

Mother Meera is not there at the time, but away in Canada on her first trip out of India.

———◇———

A GROUP OF CANADIANS invites Mother Meera to come and visit them. On September 12, 1979, she flies from Madras and arrives in Montreal, accompanied by Venkat Reddy and Adilakshmi.

This is Mother Meera's first time outside of her own country. She states that there is no great sense of difference on arriving in Canada from the East. She simply feels at home, as she did in India. Devotees gather at the CEGEP Ahuntsic auditorium on September 15, 1979. Meetings are held every Saturday night, drawing up to three hundred people, many of whom are affected deeply by the silent encounter with the small figure on the stage. They sense the perfume of her presence preceding her arrival by car, and many see her transformed into visions of their own favored deities.

———◇———

HER STAY IN CANADA lasts four months. She breaks the flight home at the beginning of 1980 to stop in Switzerland at the invitation of some Swiss devotees and then flies on to Madras.

Her car is filled with flowers as she is welcomed back to India. The fragrant load of Mother Meera, Venkat Reddy, Adilakshmi, and flowers meets with a party of four German cyclists on the street outside Mother Meera's Pondicherry home. Venkat Reddy immediately invites them to an audience with the young Divine Mother. Everyone is welcomed, and tears of wonder fill the sick man's eyes. There is something life-affirming about preaching what we love and having it loved by others.

Venkat travels up to Hyderabad to be with Jyoti for her birthday. It is the last time father and daughter will meet and the last journey he will make on his own. Her memory of him is of eyes that are demonic, of a body that stinks with sickness. There is a certain desperation in him, as he bids farewell to the sweetness of family life that is any man's dream, a world of affection and grandchildren.

He has made his choice. He returns to Pondicherry and consigns himself to Mother Meera's care.

For all of Mother Meera's apparent quietness, her life is not necessarily tranquil. On July 23, 1980, she reports:

> The Light is bursting out from me as a great tremendous sound like thunder and dazzling like bright sunlight. . . . I am sending Light like this everywhere three times a day. The Light is covering the whole Earth. When the Light leaves my body, it leaves it with such a tremendous sound that I cannot hear for two hours afterward. This process is going on.

The following month she announces that she is now a burning force, "The Mother of Fire," on account of the light she is transmitting to the earth. The earth itself is more eager for the benefits of this light than are its people.

This is the sense of power she now carries with her to the West.

CHAPTER II

On the Edge of the Forest

The four men from Germany did what many Westerners had done before them. They traded the order of their Western life for the drama of finding a spiritual master in India. It is an escape the way death is an escape, a soaring out of the world of material and emotional responsibility to reach a spiritual dimension.

Many return from India disillusioned. The people they try to take as their gurus turn out to seem shabby. For the four men the visit is wonderful. They meet Mother Meera, feel themselves changed by the touch and power of her presence, and accept their relationship with her as forming the new direction of their lives.

This new direction leads them from the light and the heat of India right back to the industrial heart of their homeland. Life with Mother Meera does not remain an escape from the world for long.

The men meet with Mother Meera as her plane makes a stop in Paris on the way back to Canada. They are free to visit her in Canada. She in turn will come and stay with them in the German city of Essen.

"I used to ask myself a question. I used to say to myself, 'Why us?'"

It is Daniel posing the question years later in the German village home he shares with Mother Meera. Actually a Slovenian who has made his home in Germany, he was one of the original four to visit her in Pondicherry.

"Why did Mother choose us to come and stay with, when there were so many others in the world? Then when I looked at it, I saw that there were not so many others like us, not so many others who were prepared to give up everything."

He laughs. He is a steady man, whose laughter comes from below a thick brown mustache where it has been hiding. People wake a little when he is around, knowing a joke will soon be cracked about them or about himself.

"We gave up everything," Daniel says. "All four of us. Beer, television, cigarettes, everything that costs money. We just worked and saved, worked and saved, so we could get the house ready in time."

"There is something . . ." Mother Meera declares on the car ride from the airport during her first moments in Germany. It is one of her typical statements, in that those who hear it are left to complete it for themselves.

She is brought to Essen along with Venkat and Adilakshmi, and Daniel moves his bed to the cellar to make room for them. Audience is given every evening, and devotees come from Canada and Italy as well as Germany. The stay is brief, only four weeks. There is trouble with the landlord, which means they will all have to move.

Mother Meera heads back to Canada for a while, but before leaving she surprises them all.

"I feel at home here," she says.

=◇=

Mother Meera is not so at home in Canada. Immigration authorities detain the trio at the airport for some time. Devotees also begin to question aspects of Mother Meera's personal life. As a guest in their homes, she resents the intimate way in which her life is being examined. She has no privacy anymore.

Venkat also becomes very ill and Canadian health regulations do not permit him to be covered for the cost of extensive treatment. It is clear that Mother Meera has no long-term future in the country.

Before leaving Canada for the last time, Venkat Reddy prompts the foundation of the Mother Meera Society. Its mission is to prepare for Mother Meera's return to North America one day. The party of three then heads back to India, with a scheduled stay in Germany en route.

=◇=

A house in the village of Kleinmaischeid is lent for Mother Meera's visit to Germany in October 1981. A swift car ride from the cities of Köln and Koblenz, yet tucked into the pastoral landscape of Germany, the house suits them all well.

"Once a week I would come to the town to do the shopping," Daniel remembers. "It was like entering another world, so noisy, so busy. I was always glad to get back home."

Kleinmaischeid curves its streets and houses across the ridge of a hill, which runs at its highest point into a thickness of forest. German forest means hunting land, and houses are decorated with sets of antlers and portraits of deer and huntsmen and hounds. A miniature Calvary stands beneath the trees at a fork in the road that climbs up through fields, Jesus Christ cast in iron and set on his cross between the two thieves. A little farther up the road a colored pietà set in a shrine shows his body in the arms of his mother.

A little higher still, at the crossroads at the center of the village, we reach another sculpture. This memorial to the dead of the world wars sits in a trim garden. Opposite it is 49 Hauptstrasse, the new home of Mother Meera. There are gardens behind its walls and views that look out across the forests of the Westerwald. A road drops down behind the house to a well-tended forest walkway, where a nature trail is filled with the sounds of rushing streams.

The house is furnished with whatever was being thrown out of other homes in the area. A devotee who remembers the time describes it with a giggle as a "hippie household."

Mother Meera, Adilakshmi, and Venkat make their home on the third floor of the Kleinmaischeid house. Audience is given daily in a room on the second floor, starting the very day of Mother Meera's arrival. The only pictures on the walls are of Sri Aurobindo and Sweet Mother. Mother Meera sits on the most respectable of the old sofas while devotees come to kneel before her.

Letters arrive from around the world. Adilakshmi is teaching literacy and foreign languages to Mother Meera, and many of these letters from devotees are used for lessons. They are read in the original language and then translated. When Mother Meera does not know the language, she listens just as intently. If there is a mistake in translation she points it out, and those who know both languages check and discover that she is right.

Coal and wood fires burn to provide the house's only heating. The winter is severe, temperatures reaching down to touch minus 20 degrees Celsius. New devotees start appearing, mainly drawn from the nearby cities of Köln and Koblenz by whispers passing through the Transcendental Meditation (TM) community, but Mother Meera is not looking for an increased number of visitors. She allows devotees to tell their best friends, but asks that word of her coming not be spread more swiftly than that.

Once, when the snow is especially thick, only Daniel is left in the house to come before Mother Meera at the appointed hour.

He is invited upstairs to a room made warm by a fire, and Mother Meera holds his head in her hands for twenty minutes.

"But only the first minute is for me and my work," she advises him. "The rest is for you."

Ten people gather in the audience room for the celebration of Mother Meera's twenty-first birthday on December 26. It seems like quite a crowd.

VENKAT REDDY IS NOW VERY ILL. He is hospitalized in Bonn for six months. His condition thereafter requires regular trips to the hospital for dialysis, and the German health system accepts him as a patient. It is clear that he is too ill to return to India.

In the spring of 1982 a dual marriage is arranged in which Mother Meera and Adilakshmi each take one of the devotees in the household as a husband. Mother Meera marries Herbert Bednarz. The nature of the marriage is never explained and is made public knowledge only some ten years later. It is presumed that the marriage is not a conventional one. It is certainly an unconventional step for a young Indian woman to have taken, presuming that the initiative was hers. Adilakshmi's and Mother Meera's marriages to German citizens serve to take away insecurities about their continued residence in Germany. The story that Venkat Reddy is Mother Meera's uncle means that he too can live the rest of his life untroubled by fears of deportation.

Tales are told in India by those who claim to have heard Mother Meera shouting at her mother. She accused her mother of neglect, of failing to find her a decent match when she was of marriageable age. Such stories can only remain as gossip, since Mother Meera ignores most questions about her personal life. She encourages facts to be wiped from her personal biography and replaced with a public myth. As information such as her marriage leaks out, devotees are left to adjust to it as best they can.

Life feels good in the home in Kleinmaischeid. Summers in the area are marked by a rich burgeoning of fruit. Apples, pears, plums, cherries, and walnuts move from bud to blossom, then swell into ripeness. After a year in the area and a round of its seasons, there is little urgency to move elsewhere. However, the tenancy of the house comes to an end at the end of 1982 and the group has to move on.

CHAPTER 12

The Valley Home

On Mother Meera's birthday near the close of 1982 she is driven to Frankfurt. A celebration is arranged by a group from the TM movement who are attempting to start up a community in the city. About one hundred people are invited to a public audience with Mother Meera. Their faces register shock when she walks into the hall. She is accompanied by her band of German men, who are not the sort of holy retinue that is expected. These men thump themselves down in their seats still smelling of tobacco from their quick smoke outdoors.

The audience is given silently. For thirty minutes Mother Meera sits and looks along each of the rows. The meditators then stand to receive their gift of a small black-and-white photograph of Mother Meera printed especially for the occasion and return to their seats as Mother Meera gazes among their rows for thirty minutes more.

In a few days' time the lease on the house in Kleinmaischeid will come to an end. Mother Meera and those who live with her will be homeless, but the Transcendental Meditators have found a house for her, so the problems of accommodation are over. This will be a "TM house," special to their community, and they will be honored to have Mother Meera at the center of their group.

She declines the offer. She does not wish to be part of any narrow spiritual or religious association.

The scenic beauty of the Westerwald suits her. It is also possible to live there and be within easy reach of the international airport at Frankfurt, an important consideration with regard to the visitors from around the world who are expected in the future. A possible home is found in the village of Thalheim, about an hour and a half's drive north of Frankfurt. The name translates as "Valley Home," which pleases Venkat, since he has long dreamed of a home in a valley. Its address is 4 Langgasse. It needs a lot of work, which brings it to a price they can all afford if the men share a mortgage.

At Christmastime Adilakshmi wraps herself up warmly and takes her wares to the marketplace in Limburg. In her stall is a selection of lampshades decorated with flowers she stenciled herself and tassels tied by Mother Meera. Most of the sales are to devotees.

Daniel leaves the household for a while to join another spiritual community; his doubts about Mother Meera, he says, lie in his head rather than his heart. She telephones him to invite him back, and he returns. Much of the financial burden of running the house is now his. He pays for it through his work cleaning and maintaining roofs and gutters. Calls to his business and to Mother Meera come on the one phone line, and a shout brings Mother Meera down from the floor above when she is needed.

Daniel lives on the middle floor. Above him is the suite that houses Adilakshmi, Venkat, Herbert, and the living room. Mother Meera climbs up a small ladder and through a hatch door to her own bedroom in the attic.

Public audience is given in a room on the first floor. There are seldom more than ten people at any gathering. After fifteen minutes or so Adilakshmi disappears, to come back at the end holding a tray loaded with tea and cakes. Newcomers who can afford it are asked to pay twenty-five deutsche marks for the tea as a way of funding the household.

In April and May of that year the effects on Mother Meera's body of her work in bringing down light are obvious to everyone in the household. This particular light is seen as manifesting love on earth. As Mother Meera's body channels it during these months, her body is cut off from its normal senses. It shakes, her legs and arms flail. For the first few days this only happens between midnight and six in the morning. Then the pressure mounts, the descent of light is continual, and at times the pain is so extreme Mother Meera becomes unconscious. She comes around from this state long enough to refuse the services of a doctor, then resumes her coma. Eventually the feeling of love that comes with the light so fills the house that the devotees' concern is replaced by a feeling of joy.

"MANY DEVOTEES WROTE to thank Mother when the Berlin Wall came down," Adilakshmi says. She is explaining the esoteric reasons for Mother Meera's choice of Germany as her home. "They know it was her work. You can put that in your book."

Mother Meera gives a devotee a direct if far from fulsome answer as to why she came to Germany: "Because of the two world wars."

Adilakshmi says that Mother Meera has come "to the heart of the wound," to a country in great need of healing from its recent history. There are many Jews among her followers who make the trip to Germany and in so doing overcome many of their horrors of the country and its recent history. Also when a country suffers two such huge defeats, it loses the opportunity to grieve for its dead. There is no balm of victory. Instead of pride, there is shame. There is much healing to be done.

Adilakshmi agrees that the presence of the town of Hadamar just six miles away is an important factor in understanding Mother Meera's choice of home.

———◇———

A DARK, TURRETED CASTLE broods over Hadamar. Its stone grows lighter as one approaches it up a hill. It is an international school and home of the Limburg Cathedral choir.

The psychiatric hospital at Hadamar across to the right includes a much more innocuous-looking building. It was used for genetic experimentation and a program of enforced sterilization prior to the Second World War. It was subsequently the last of six Nazi death stations to be set up, five of them in Germany and one in Austria. Between January and August 1941, 10,071 people were killed in its gas chambers—the mentally ill, Jews, homosexuals, soldiers injured in war, people who, it was decided, had no fit part to play in the German Reich.

The use of gas chambers was then moved to Poland and deaths were administered in Hadamar through pills and injections. Between 1942 and 1945, 4,817 patients were admitted into the hospital, of whom 4,422 died. They were buried in mass graves on the hilltop behind.

A suite of rooms, some showing an exhibition about the atrocities, has been installed on the ground floor of the hospital building. Below this room is the rough concrete cellar and the small white-tiled room that formed the gas chamber. Like an institutional shower room, it could squeeze in about sixty people at a time.

People were weighed, measured, and photographed in the antechamber. Doctors would invent reasons for death and fill out their death certificates. Then they were passed into the chamber into which carbon-monoxide gas was fed from two cylinders. Six stone tables were set up in the next room for dissection of the bodies, and from there trolleys ran the few meters to the crematorium ovens.

Pictures in the exhibition show portraits of some of the patients and the smoke they turned into, which belched day and night from the stack above the ovens to rain as soot upon the town.

There is a photo of the smiling young men and women who worked at the hospital too. They need prayers as those who died need prayers.

At the top of the hill behind the hospital is a graveyard. It is now marked with Jewish memorials. There is an iron gate in the far wall. Through it is a view across fields to the houses of the village of Dorndorf above Mother Meera's valley.

❖

AT FOUR O'CLOCK in the morning Adilakshmi rises to prepare breakfast for Venkat Reddy. He is helped downstairs and an ambulance arrives at six to carry him away for the morning's dialysis. When he returns, he reclines on the couch in the audience room, semiconscious, before making the move back up the flights of stairs. Mother Meera supports him from one side as he walks, someone else from the other.

He is comforted by a vision he once had in which thousands gathered in a great hall to be with Mother Meera. This is assurance that his goal of bringing her to the world's attention is secured, even though the full reality lies some years ahead. Now he is old before his time, sick beyond his years, and the body that has carried him so far has to be carried by others. He does not wish to share Mother Meera anymore. He no longer wants to talk about her, to promote her, but simply to be with her. When she wanders from his sight even for a moment he calls for her return, and when she comes back he cries tears of relief and joy.

He cries for Jyoti too, cries for the love that was lost between a father and a daughter. When he is no longer able to direct the pen for himself, Adilakshmi writes letters to Jyoti for him. Packages are sent to her, now a language professor in France, but she gives instructions to return them unopened. She is located by phone and the receiver is passed to Venkat. Jyoti hears a tearful man who speaks Telugu, but otherwise there is nothing in the voice that suggests this is the man she remembers. She suspects an impostor has been brought in to mimic her father and hangs up the phone.

Mother Meera leaves Germany to spend time with a devotee, the Prince of Thurn and Taxis, at Duino Castle near Trieste in Italy. A dapper and frail character with a waxed mustache, he was introduced to her through Jean-Marc, the Canadian who was the first to receive her touch and gaze at the gatherings in her Pondicherry home. The prince will not live long himself. Mother Meera will return to Duino Castle the following November to be at his bedside as he dies. For now she must leave him, because telephone calls to Germany reveal that Venkat is in great distress at Mother Meera's absence and that his condition is worsening.

Mother Meera returns as Venkat prepares to leave her home for the last time. He spends a day listening to his favorite Indian devotional songs and is then transferred to a hospital bed in Limburg. For a week he lies in intensive care. Devotees see his body as shining, and Mother Meera catches the first scents of a fragrance that others will notice after his death. On June 19, 1985, Mother Meera announces that his body is like any other man's and that his essence has departed. The following day he dies.

⟡

ADILAKSHMI WRITES how, for days after Venkat's death, a severe pain enters Mother Meera's heart at four o'clock in the afternoon and stays there for hours. Nausea fills her stomach, and whenever she lowers her head, all her organs seem about to vomit from her. She walks as though through space, with little sense of contact with the earth as her head spins. When she tends the soil of the fresh grave, her hand breaks out in sores.

Venkat appears to her. She focuses her grief in a sequence of watercolor paintings that show his passage through the afterlife in the company of divine light and divine mothers. Some of these she hands as gifts to devotees and others are sold to devotees to produce income. The body of Venkat has gone from the house. In its place is her sorrow.

Life is an acceptance of the physical condition, and grief is a part of that condition. When one body dies, another body grieves. Grief is an appreciation of loss.

Venkat's body is buried rather than cremated, for Mother Meera says the vibrations of such a body survive for a time after death.

In *The Mother* we find the following explanation from Mother Meera:

> Our body is an instrument and servant to our consciousness. Our consciousness is quite free from the body and will function according to its condition. It will work in and beyond time, in and beyond space, in darkness as in light, in form as in formlessness. The soul is free from limits. Our field of consciousness is full of action, without words. It bears an ocean of knowledge. It is without rest.
>
> Our body moves here as a machine, our consciousness moves everywhere, without hindrance. Whatever is accomplished with the body without a higher consciousness is purely nominal and has no value. But with the aid of the higher consciousness its work is important to the Divine Play. Nothing can affect our consciousness, which moves and acts without the body. There will therefore be no change in its action after death, for if the body vanishes, our consciousness does not disappear. Within or without the body, we are always in consciousness.

Mother Meera's life and work go on. Though Venkat Reddy is buried, Mother Meera and Adilakshmi sense that he is with them as fully as ever.

⎯⎯◇⎯⎯

A BOOK PUBLISHED IN FRENCH on Mother Meera brings in the first wave of new nationalities. The French come, attracted by a link they see with Sweet Mother and Sri Aurobindo, followed by the Belgians and the Dutch.

The small audience room is outgrown and in December 1985 the meetings move up to the second floor. A wall is knocked down and the main upstairs room opened to the staircase. On busy days, especially Mother Meera's birthday, devotees sit on the stairs going up to the next floor and Mother Meera's living space, and even all the way down two flights of stairs. The tail end of the line sits waiting in the basement kitchen.

Four photos of Mother Meera are hung in a frame, and devotees can purchase copies from Daniel. This is the beginning of the small commercial operation trading in images of Mother Meera that will help meet some of the operating costs of the house.

In January 1986 there is a temporary change of venue for the gathering of devotees. Mother Meera has had a nose operation. Even as she recovers, devotees take their turn to pass by her hospital bed and take hold of her hand.

———◇———

THE GATHERINGS for the nightly audiences with Mother Meera grow bigger. Mother Meera decides to keep the house they have and also buy another one.

A large building is found in a small crescent of a street in the same village. It borders a stream, and fields rise steeply out of the valley on the far side of its garden. It was used as a storage barn and cattle shed; large barn doors fill the village-facing wall of the first floor. For many years it has been in disuse. It needs a tremendous amount of work to transform it into a home.

Mother Meera and some devotees take out a joint mortgage on the house in 1988. Together with an architect, Mother Meera devises a plan for its conversion into a three-story house with rooms for guests and a large hall for meetings.

The budget is tight. Many devotees volunteer their time, half a dozen of them also bringing in specialized skills. Mother Meera dons trousers and heavy shoes, a smock and rubber gloves, to drop her own energy into the pool of workers. Memories of that time render Mother Meera as a dynamo, an example of swift, steady, and expert work, from hauling goods at ground level to fixing the tiles on the roof.

The cordless phone rings while she is swinging spadeloads of sand into the cement mixer. She dusts off her hands and goes around the corner to answer it, giving details of audience times in response to an inquiry, and then comes back to her labor. Some days with less than an hour to spare Mother Meera downs tools, heads home for a shower, and then appears transfigured for the evening's gathering.

She takes a power drill to walls, lays mortar for a brick wall on the third floor, and fixes plates to the chimney.

Marc, a young Belgian butcher of unusual strength, still comes to this remodeled house as a guest on many weekends. He rolls large slabs of steaks into the frying pan for his dinner, and cracks cartons of eggs into bowls to whisk up into pancakes to feed every devotee in residence. He tells his own favorite story of the time spent working on the house.

Only he and Mother Meera are on site. She calls him to one side of an extra large cement mixer and takes hold of the other side herself. Together they lift it up the stairs to the second floor, and then when it cannot fit through the door, they bring it back down again.

Many find it hard to see beyond Marc's size and strength. In this incident with the concrete mixer, Mother Meera shows she can more than match his strength with her own. The strength is not extraordinary to her. Sheer size does not help to enter any door, as the concrete mixer proves. She welcomes Marc, lets him in through the door of her own home, on account of all of his good qualities and not just his size and strength. This shared act proves to Marc that he is loved and accepted for himself. It is the fundamental parable in his life.

Female devotees prepare and supply snacks throughout each day of building work, Adilakshmi sweeping down at the close of work with a tray of Indian tea and cakes. Mother Meera slices the cake, takes the smallest piece for herself, and hands slabs of the rest to the men all around her.

Devotees have formed themselves into bands, the men working as laborers and the women in the kitchen. The working pattern of the house has drawn a dividing line between male and female tasks. Mother Meera skips neatly over the line to side with the men.

━━━◇━━━

A BOOK IS BEING WRITTEN about Mother Meera during this time. Andrew Harvey began it in 1982, the manuscript pages piling high in the basement room beside the kitchen in the Langgasse house, which was reserved for his occasional visits. In 1989 the book is nearing completion. He wishes to introduce her to America and arranges an invitation from Hobart and William Smith College in Geneva, New York, where he sometimes teaches.

A small group of around ten gather to meet Mother Meera and her followers when they arrive at JFK airport in New York. Dressed in a navy sari and purple sweater, tired and a little bedraggled from the flight, Mother Meera conjures different reactions.

A devotee who knows her from Germany describes her as "absolutely luminous," smiling and shining as a still center against the shifting backdrop of suitcases and people.

Another man, who has heard his friends preach their love of Mother Meera and has come to see her for the first time, notes her short height, her tiredness, and that she looks no one in the eye. She climbs into a limousine and is ferried in a motorcade to the apartment on New York's Upper West Side where she will stay. Her first audience, planned for an hour after her arrival, is canceled due to illness.

This visit is to be the culmination of a celebration of the Divine Mother at Hobart and William Smith College. Posters pinned around the halls announce the arrival of Mother Meera as guru, teacher, and goddess. The display embarrasses some of those who are with her.

Mother Meera wears an emerald green and white sari for the occasion and looks impossibly young. She appears before a gathering in the garden, then moves through to a large study room where her usual silence is broken for a public question-and-answer session.

Adilakshmi sits by her side as Mother Meera faces the assembly of about fifty people, many of them academics. Their questions sometimes take a while, unraveling slowly from their intellects. Mother Meera answers in short phrases.

The session lasts about forty-five minutes. Many of Mother Meera's responses on this day form the basis for her 1991 book *Answers*.

Not all of the questions are preserved in that book. One man wishes to know what he should eat to ensure his spiritual salvation. The question makes no sense to Mother Meera. The man repeats it, and Adilakshmi translates.

"Eat what you like," Mother Meera answers.

Everyone laughs.

Those who have known Mother Meera without knowing her voice are thrilled to hear it now. Accompanying her to this gathering of academics is like taking a loved one home to meet the parents. They come away quite proud of her performance.

———◇———

ADILAKSHMI LAUGHS when she remembers advice given to Mother Meera about New Yorkers. Their temperament is such that they can only sit in silence for a maximum of half an hour, Mother Meera is told, but she declares New Yorkers are like all people everywhere. They will be gathered in her silence for as long as she holds them there.

About fifty people are gathered by word of mouth and assemble in a side chapel of the Cathedral of St. John the Divine for

Mother Meera's first public appearance in America. Those who are new to her are surprised to find themselves standing as she makes her appearance, though no such instructions have been given. An actor who is there comments on the extraordinarily subdued nature of her entrance, as though she prefers not to be noticed at all.

The following night Mother Meera gives one of two audiences at high-society locations in Manhattan. The hostess of one on Fifth Avenue remembers returning to her home after the guests had already arrived. She is astonished to find the largest pile of footwear she has ever seen, much of it curious, gathered in her hall. The food is excellent and the setting exquisite; great paintings line the high walls of the apartment and immense Buddhas meditate on the floor. Mother Meera sits at the head of the table and fields the many social questions with her smile, and silence.

Before leaving the city, she takes the ferry out to Liberty Island with a small group of devotees, is carried by elevator up the Statue of Liberty, and wanders around inside the statue's head. In one direction she looks out across the Hudson and into America. In the other she looks out across the Atlantic and back to Europe.

═◇═

ON HER RETURN TO THALHEIM, her car travels over petal-strewn roads while flags fly to either side of the street and a brass band marches ahead of her. Her arrival coincides with a Roman Catholic procession that is passing through the village. The new house is decorated with balloons on which devotees have written their messages of love and welcome. Her eyes are seen to water at the sight.

CHAPTER 13

The Indian Base

With two homes in Germany, Mother Meera feels free to divert funds to the acquisition of real estate back in India. In April 1988 she visits the country, choosing Adilakshmi's hometown of Madanapalle as her own. It is in her home state of Andhra Pradesh, her native language of Telugu is spoken there, and the town's altitude gives it a pleasant climate in the summer months. Property is duly selected, and construction work begins on a new house.

The nearest large city is Bangalore, the capital of the neighboring state of Karnataka. People are fond of Bangalore. Some distance above the scorching heat of the plains, it is known as the garden city of India. Bullock carts, buses, and lorries share the single-lane road north from the city. The driving is civilized and mercifully silent of blaring horns. The road passes through mango plantations, small thatched settlements that fringe the base of the mountains, splashes of reflective color that are lakes, corridors of palm trees, and rock formations that bulge from fields to look like fat, recumbent gods spilling grapes from their mouths. This is a soft, village India, where people stroll easy-paced and come out to the road at dusk to sit and enjoy its warmth.

A high archway of old stone stands to the right of the highway and signals that the idyllic spread of countryside is coming to an end. This is Colony Gate. Its lilac paint flakes onto the dust of an assembly ground where no one assembles anymore. A wide pond lies in front of it, thick with the green of algae; the thatch-roofed shacks of basic homes built on its banks look picturesque beneath the trees. Mosquitoes lift as a cloud from the water's surface at dusk and drift off in search of blood. This lilac imperial archway was a futile attempt at grandeur. Even the main road passes it by with barely a sideward glance.

Thirty thousand people live in Madanapalle, yet it is hard to conceive of it as a town at all. These Indian towns do not come with any civic scale. There is no likes of a town hall or plaza to provide a focal point. People scooped up mud and baked bricks to form the walls of houses, and these houses gathered together to form a village. Then village after village sprouted up, the lanes of one merging with the lanes of another so it is impossible to tell where one begins and the other ends. They congeal into the size, though not the shape, of a city.

Madanapalle is marked as a dot in the bottom left corner of any map of the state. The railway passes some miles to the north, and this town started by some stubborn will of its own. Early supplies were brought in by bullock cart, and it kept on growing. The maps show it as existing without explaining why. Its winding streets are formed into neighborhoods by individual temples that draw worshipers from the surrounding homes or attract people to their principal deity. People step out through the temple gates and their lives intermingle once again.

Traveling down a side road at the outer edge of town, beside the Colony Gate, we meet one of the very few street signs in the whole district. Owning what is by far the largest house on the end of the street, Mother Meera had the chance to name it. The blue sign reads "Paramatman Way" ("Paramatman" being her favored name for the supreme divinity that is God) and points toward her home.

The grounds are surrounded by granite walls and the entranceway guarded by a wrought-iron gateway some three meters high. An inscription chiseled into one of the gateposts announces that the whole house stands as a memorial to Venkat Reddy.

The chief of police drives out sometimes to visit the house that grows deep within the walls. He stands in the gateway and looks down the drive, through an avenue of coconut palms, to a house that grows in magnificence beyond anything he could aspire to. This is the largest, grandest house ever to have appeared in this portion of India.

The garden is flourishing, with neat rows of vegetables, maize, and chilies arranged between the mango and papaya trees. Money can buy construction materials, but nature needs time, so Mother Meera designed this garden and left it to grow through the years. The house itself is incomplete. Its color is the gray stone of its unfinished blocks, reaching up three stories.

The first floor is closest to completion. Its walls are bare plaster and the furniture is primitive scrubbed wood. The house provides the essential rudiments of living with few hints of luxury. Many people live between these rooms, though it is hard to understand quite how. Their few possessions are hidden away in some neat order, so when the residents leave, there is scarcely a trace of their occupancy. They seem like visitors passing through.

They are about thirteen people in all and form Mother Meera's extended family. There are her two surviving sisters, their children, her three young cousins whose mother died, her parents, her uncle, and her brother, Raju, who handles the estate's everyday management. Movements between this house and Chandepalle, the village of her birth, keep this population in some state of flux.

The family gathers in the intimacy of each other's company and finds the flavor of their lives in each other, rather than in ornaments, comfort, or space. This one story of the house they all inhabit witnesses life at a simple level. The rest of the house is an oddity, a monument of some sort, that stands around them without any obvious function in their lives.

Below them is a basement that has a ceiling high enough to turn the room into a cube. At some future date it could hold gatherings of the size known in Germany, with an adjacent room that could be used for the sale of publications and photographs. The floor is of marble brought from Rajasthan; pink- and gray-veined, it will polish to the shine of a mirror.

Above them the second floor holds bedrooms with bathrooms attached. Some windows are glazed, others are simply open spaces. Electric wires course across the concrete floors waiting to be fitted. This floor is presumably designed for visitors.

The top floor is still waiting to take the shape of rooms, its walls and pillars simply offering support to the roof. If it follows the pattern of Mother Meera's German homes, it will provide the accommodation for herself, her husband, and Adilakshmi.

A telephone sits on a bureau in the largest first-floor room, which has a table and so is used for dining. When it rings the family gathers around it excitedly, for it is likely to be either Mother Meera or Adilakshmi. They call from Germany regularly. They seek news of the family's welfare and financial situation and deliver instructions regarding the lives of the family members and the workings of the estate.

Two statues of gods, both painted gaily, stand out in the open air in the corner of the yard. One is the dancing elephant god, Ganesh, the other the monkey god, Hanuman.

═══◇═══

AT TWO THOUSAND FEET, the town has cooler summer temperatures than other towns in the state. Hills are some kilometers distant, a fine horizon to be admired from Madanapalle's plain.

This is a green part of India. Mother Meera owns thirteen acres of farmland about twenty minutes' walk from her house.

The walk is either along the ridges raised between open fields or through a mango grove, a beautiful spot of dappled shade and scattering monkeys.

A supply of water is what makes land either rich or poor. The family bored deep into the thirteen acres and found it dry. Mother Meera came along, suggested they run pipes to a point fifty feet away and try again, and they found their main water source.

This farm is a beautiful place. A day-old calf sits, tethered and blinking, in the shade of a barn's wooden canopy. Cots are placed in the shade of mango trees, while coconut trees form a separate grove. Cows and more calves are tethered to the trees and taken in turn for a drink from the trough. Five guinea fowl move around in close formation. A rooster struts and crows while hens and chicks churn the dust with their feet. Chicks that have outgrown their beauty, gray creatures with long rangy necks, run and jump senselessly over every obstacle. A kitten sleeps in a basket. Dogs, named after characters in the American soap opera *Dallas*, collapse in the heat as tiny mangoes drop around them, pushed from the branches by a squirrel.

When Mother Meera is visiting, this is her favorite place. Visitors crowd into the courtyard of the house whenever she sits on its verandah. There are no public gatherings with scheduled times and a shared silence. Devotees and curious townsfolk come and go, chattering as they do so, and drop to their knees or lie prostrate in front of her chair as they clutch her feet in supplication. This farm is a pleasing respite from all that mad devotion. She likes to come here to sit between six and ten o'clock in the morning and then often returns once more at dusk.

Beyond the low farm buildings stretch the thirteen acres of fields. Hired hands come in for the occasional days when swift work is essential—for picking crops or planting seedlings—but otherwise the farm is entirely managed by members of Mother Meera's family. Sugarcane rises placidly out of the ground, small tomato plants struggle through their early days in irrigated channels, while acres of sunflowers bend their heads as they are filled with the weight of their seeds.

Parakeets whistle from the trees all around, each call met by banging drums and human cries. Masses of parakeets swoop in in great green flashes and harvest the seeds before they can be picked. Mother Meera's family gathers to keep them at bay, her parents and uncle patrolling different sections, yelling and rattling tin cans.

The mother, Antamma, is closest, treading barefoot through the sunflower plants to the right, her gray hair tied up behind her head, her short body trim and erect, her cotton sari tied up around her legs, and the brightness of gold rings glistening in her nose and ears. "Whoop! Whoop! Whoop!" she cries, clapping her hands to frighten off the birds.

The father, Veera, is at the far edge of the field, dressed in white, a white cloth tied around his head to keep it from the sun. A little bow-legged, a little stooped, and walking slowly, he shows more signs of age than his wife. A medallion bearing the portrait of his daughter hangs around his neck. He lets out an occasional shout and bangs a stick against a tin can.

───◇───

ADILAKSHMI LAUGHS when she remembers taking a picnic to eat near the house. She did not know which way to turn, how she could settle on the ground. In one direction was a mosque, in another a church, in another a temple, and in another the home of Mother Meera. Whichever way she sat she would have to turn her back on one of them, and she did not wish to be discourteous in such a way.

It is telling, she feels, that Mother Meera's home is at the center of places of worship in the Hindu, Christian, and Muslim traditions.

Once Adilakshmi and Venkat adorned Mother Meera with flowers and performed a full *puja*, the Hindu ceremony of worship, in front of her. Once too Mother Meera sat at the center of the celebration of the goddess Durga in the Shiva temple next door to her house, leading the *puja* that was also directed toward herself. This was a joy for all those who could share in the occasion, but it was totally unplanned.

"It was a mistake," Adilakshmi explains. "The priest asked us to sponsor the day. Mother agreed. Then when the day came, the priest insisted that Mother be at the center of the worship. Mother is kind. She does not like to disappoint."

Coated in fresh lilac paint, this temple to Shiva is kept in an excellent state of repair. The *lingam*, a small column of stone that represents the god himself, is housed in a dark recess and attended by his constant companion, a stone sculpture of a bull called Nandi. The temple's side annex, opened in 1964, is light and airy. Three small, dark, garlanded idols stand behind an iron grille. Though they represent the gods Rana, Lakshmana, and Sita, the priest is happier to promote the fact that he holds a service three times a day to three of the female deities. He lights flames and speaks his holy words to honor the goddesses Durga, Lakshmi, and Saraswathi.

In her absence from India, Mother Meera's family, friends, and devotees gather at the house for two special occasions each year. One is the last day of the festival to Durga, which Mother Meera sponsors to the tune of almost thirty thousand rupees. Vast quantities of food are prepared in the house on this day to feed all who come.

The other big festivity at the house is for the celebration of Mother Meera's own birthday on December 26.

———◇———

BESIDES THE SHIVA TEMPLE, there are three other principal temples in town. One is to the monkey god, Hanuman, another is to the elephant god, Ganesh, and the third is to the Lord Venkateswara, the incarnation of the supreme god Vishnu, who once crossed this town on the way to his mountaintop home in the hills of Tirupati. A walk through Madanapalle is a walk through the lives of other major spiritual figures of the twentieth century too.

J. Krishnamurti was born in a small house just two minutes' walk from Adilakshmi's home. It is tucked away down a side street, owned by the Indian government and so likely to be preserved, but closed to visitors at the moment. From Madanapalle the boy Krishnamurti was adopted by Annie Besant of the Theosophical movement and coached into accepting the role of new messiah to the world. Eventually he declined to play this part, asking that seekers turn their attention from him to examine the potential for growth and awareness in their own lives.

The Maharishi Mahesh Yogi began his mission by teaching in a hall at the corner of Adilakshmi's street, a mission that has seen the growth of the Transcendental Meditation movement throughout the world. Adilakshmi took a mantra from the Maharishi herself, but did not feel it had the power she needed for her life.

Mother Meera lodged opposite this mission during her own early stays in the town, in the Bhajana Lodge. She would come out onto the balcony each morning and monkeys would run up to greet her. Adilakshmi's family home was just yards away along the high street, where Adilakshmi's father ran his clothing business.

      —◇—

ADILAKSHMI'S FATHER, Olati Venkataram Krishnamurti, is a regular visitor to the Mother Meera household. He is a popular man, reaching into an inexhaustible bag of boiled sweets that he carries with him at all times to distribute to all he meets. Despite the deaths of both his sons, his spirits are high.

He appears one evening on the back of the motorbike of Mother Meera's brother, Raju, and climbs up the stairs to meet us and have his photograph taken. He is able to sit absolutely still for the camera's longest exposure. In his crisp white Indian dress and his fawn vest, with his upright posture, neat and glowing scalp, and direct gaze, he is perfect material for any portrait of a fiery old Indian gentleman.

He fires out his English sentences to announce he cannot speak English—once an independence fighter, always an independence fighter. When he speaks in Telugu it is hard too, for Raju cannot understand his philosophical language.

"India must be forward. Independent. Forward in the world," he shouts, clenching his fist to hammer the point against the air.

He keeps unclasping the fist to shake hands.

"Adilakshmi says we must all be friendly, but all families fight, everywhere," he says, then remembers. "But I am friendly with everyone."

He grips his friends in a hug.

"I am eighty-five." He holds out his forearm to be felt. It is as strong as he promises it to be.

When he speaks of visiting the holy man Ramana Maharshi at his ashram at the foot of the sacred mountain Arunachala and looking into the sage's eyes in silence, he demonstrates the look he received. His eyes are a little milky, the whites are yellow, and the pupils hazel, but the gaze is fixed and steady.

He remembers his journey to find Adilakshmi at the Aurobindo ashram. His own memory of her flight from home is that it was a reaction to her sister-in-law's insistence that Adilakshmi get a job. When she refused to come home with him, the family disowned her for some years, but when she began to take care of Mother Meera's financial affairs, she came back into favor.

His farewell blessing comes as a close, warm hug, once to the right and once to the left.

"God is in there," he says, tapping his friend's chest. "In the head. God is in there too. And there." He taps his own chest. "That is why we hug. We give each other God."

He hugs again, once to the right, once to the left.

"God is everywhere," he says, then breaks into a strong, clear song in Telugu that sings of God's omnipresence.

"God is in my stick." He taps his walking stick. "If I don't have it, I fall over."

He taps his way out of the room and down the stairs and gives candies to the women gathered on the front steps. With the highest step as his stage, he stops and sings another fine song. His voice is praised for its strength.

"Much power," he says, and sings again, clapping his hands in rhythm, then holding them still to clasp the final note as a prayer.

He is off to Tirupati at four o'clock in the morning, on his regular pilgrimage to stare at the image of Lord Venkateswara. Walking out through the front gates, he climbs onto the back of Raju's motorbike, hooks his walking stick over the back of his shirt collar, holds on to the seat with his left hand as he waves with his right, and is whisked into the gathering darkness.

—◇—

ADILAKSHMI'S BEST FRIEND from girlhood visits with her husband. They are both teachers who work in the town. She met Adilakshmi for the first time in many years at the Shiva temple in 1991. The foundations of the house were then being dug. In 1992 she and her husband were introduced to Mother Meera.

As teachers this couple take an interest in the education of the children of the family. In thanks, Mother Meera has decreed that they receive some milk each day from the cows on the family's farm. This is duly delivered, though in the concern for Mother Meera's welfare during one of her visits to her Indian home the milk was forgotten for a few days.

Mother Meera asked about the milk delivery while eating her dinner and was told it had been neglected.

She vomited up all the food she had eaten and said she would never eat again until the matter was set to rights. She left the table. Within half an hour she had gone to the couple's home to express her concern for their welfare and complained how her family could not be trusted to look after even such little things without her keeping an eye on them.

The couple are thankful to Mother Meera too for the fine marriage made by their son. They attribute their son's good fortune to the grace that comes from their own devotion. Their daughter was also helped in a most practical way. Away at medical college, she hated the free life she had in her dormitory and wished to return home. Mother Meera counseled her to stay and so overcome her fears and telephoned her weekly to speak with her and encourage her. The girl is often comforted in dreams by both Mother Meera and Adilakshmi, who appear in golden light.

The couple look out from the balcony and over the neighboring land. They wish to buy land for themselves nearby, so they can live closer.

MOTHER MEERA FURTHER SHOWED her concern for education when her younger brother, Raju, was restless in adolescence and having difficulties at home. There was no education beyond sixth grade in the village, so she arranged for him to stay at the home of a schoolteacher in a nearby town, where he could continue his studies. To encourage him, they exchanged weekly letters between Germany and India.

Now, even in his position as head of the Indian household, he is still busy studying. He writes to Mother Meera to let her know the date and time of every examination, and he begins each test by writing two names at the top of the paper to bring him luck. One name is Ganesh, the elephant god; the other name is Mother Meera.

A COUPLE OF WOMEN step in through the iron gateway and begin to circle each other on the paved driveway. One is old, the other young, one tall, the other short, in plain cotton saris of dark colors that cling to their bodies like second skins; their movements are a sinuous winding dance.

Silver bells shake on chains about their wrists as their arms reach far above their heads, their hands wind separate dances that mirror the dance that plays beneath them, and their fingers trill out rhythms in the air.

Then separate waves of motion set in, waves that pass between their bodies as they step around each other, each woman bending from the waist so that their dance becomes a circle spinning on its side. Their hands reach in to clap at the circle's center, the wrists' silver bells jangle excitement at the rhythm, and the women sing. The words of their song patter as fast as the barefoot steps of their dance. The tune reaches high and low, high and low, following the stretching of their bodies. Their shrill voices cut through the hot air, voices that can draw audiences from across crowded marketplaces.

The women, in fact, are two of India's millions of eunuchs known as *hijras*. Sexless men who adorn themselves in women's clothing, they bring the wildness of their lives to celebrate births and weddings throughout the land. *Hijras* who dance for a living, the sinuous feminine eunuchs dance in the courtyard of a divine mother's spectacular home.

—◇—

AN OLD WOMAN, dressed in black, her white hair hanging loose like an old wedding veil, stands in the road. Her hands reach through the grille of the iron gate and hang there, the skin of her fingers fitting loosely round the bones.

Her mouth gapes small and black.

"Ma!" she calls, and the mouth closes again. "Ma!"

Her body is still except for her mouth.

"Ma!" the call comes, every twenty seconds or so. "Ma!"

—◇—

THE LARGER HOUSES in an Indian town attract many visitors such as these. Hands accept rupees and drop them into purses in the hidden folds of saris, and the woman and *hijras* vanish.

One moment they are there, like heat haze that shimmers above a road. The next moment they are gone.

——◇——

TOWARD THE CLOSE OF DAY young men appear, to sit on the earth in the shade of trees or recline on the broad sofa of a branch. Others trace the geometry of the land with their bare feet, walking the ridges between the rice fields. Their heads are bent toward their books, and their lips move around the words they are reading.

Whole books are breathed in the murmur of their voices. The days of the school exams are approaching. Students have to learn passages by heart so they can spill them across examination pages when the chance arises.

Beyond them, blue buses speed along the main road, their rooftops dense with passengers. Young men sprout from every window, hanging on to the bus with one hand while the hot wind dries the sweat from their faces.

——◇——

JULIE AND CHARLIE, two dogs from Mother Meera's farm, come back to the house in the evening. This is the lazy time of day when bodies stir but still are languid. Charlie mounts Julie in the courtyard, the brown dog on the white. She stands patiently through all his lazy thrusting. When the moment comes to disengage, Charlie tugs as Julie stands, but still they stick together.

Their efforts to separate are funny and somehow tender. Charlie wheelbarrows Julie around the coconut palms as she curls her head around to nuzzle their genitals loose and free.

Patiently, after fifteen anxious minutes, she succeeds.

Their dance complete, the two dogs collapse in separate patches of shade.

——◇——

LARGE MILLSTONES ARE HEAVED into position and the house reverberates as they are turned to grind tamarind seeds into powder. Crickets spark into life with the sunset and mosquitoes stream in with the breeze. They drift and land around Mother Meera's home, the females buzzing on the fuel of human blood. Creation is at its most obviously beautiful in these hours before sunset. The sun sinks below its white flare and the land shines back through infinite shades of green.

Birds fill every level of the sky. Pigeons dart around the roof. Parrots swoop in green curves of flight to perch with shrill cries. A kingfisher shrieks with the efforts of pulling itself up to a TV aerial, rests, then speeds in a turquoise flash down to the fields. Egrets make their pure white solo journeys across the center of the picture.

And large gray kites, a mass of the birds, spiral around and around, the highest merely distant specks in a funnel that reaches the heavens.

CHAPTER 14

Glimpses of Home

Tamarind leaves hang from strings across the tops of doorways. This marks the day as the first day of the local new year. It is a festival, a good day for visiting. People are at home.

Mukunda Reddy is a village elder and the foremost of those in the village of Mother Meera's birth who maintain ties with her. His home is spacious, essentially made up of one room but with furniture arranged and walls bent around corners so that there are many separate pockets of space to contain people. The place is well peopled with young and old, big and small, each appearing with a smile and fading away again as they go about their business. The beams of the house are painted sky blue and carved with flowers, bright tracks above their heads for the people to follow around.

The beams are not far above Mukunda's head. He is tall, his hair and clothing white. He is the pillar that the lives of everyone else are centered around. He gives instructions to keep the others on course, while his own movements are composed of a slowly shifting stillness.

To a bee, a beehive might feel something like his home.

He sits himself down, leaning forward so that his arms rest on his knees, and studies his fingers as they interlace to bind his hands together.

This operation complete, he looks up and speaks of his wish.

Mukunda is a politician. He does not speak of his wish as being his own. It is a wish for the village, and it is the heart's desire of someone very dear to Mother Meera.

It is the wish of Venkat Reddy.

Throughout his life one of Venkat's chief aims, Mukunda declares, was to promote his village of Chandepalle and all those that surround it. He was always bringing state officials on visits so that the village might have first call when aid was handed out. If he went as far afield as Madras, he was likely to return with government ministers in tow.

The last letter Mukunda received from him, while Venkat was in Germany and shortly before he died, showed that this ambition for his village was with him till the end. He wrote of how he wished for Mother Meera to build an ashram in the village someday. It would be located near the water tower, and its buildings would include a wedding hall and a school.

Mukunda wrote to Mother Meera. He suggested that this was a good time for Venkat's dream to come true.

Now he would open a letter that she had sent in reply. Everyone is silent while he reads.

—◇—

THE TELEVISION IS SILENT TOO. It is set on a high table in a corner and shows an episode from a dramatized religious epic. Around the walls is a gallery of spiritual figures and Hindu deities. Sweet Mother is there, in a black-and-white photo that is signed and dedicated especially to Mukunda. The light is dim, the ink fading, the message in French and in her handwriting, and so it is hard to read. It is nice that it is there, though.

Photos of Sri Aurobindo and Sweet Mother hang in many of the village homes. They are relics of Venkat Reddy's concern that everyone he knew should come to care for the holy couple. There is a black-and-white picture of Gillala Puri, a woman saint, now dead.

There is no picture of Mother Meera in sight. Her image has yet to appear on the walls of any households in this district of her birth.

—◇—

THE LETTER FROM MOTHER MEERA is neatly scripted in Telugu. Mukunda finishes reading and looks up. He nods his head with satisfaction. He has work to do.

"Mother says yes," he says.

She also states her purchase price for the land, twelve acres behind the water tower.

—◇—

A DELEGATION GATHERS in the street, Mukunda at the head and every youngster in the village in tow.

They pass the water tower to their right, high above them on its stilts, painted an orange overlaid with black graffiti. The new Mother Meera ashram is to be nearby, and they are going to inspect the available land.

Mother Meera states that she does not want ashrams, and in Germany her Western devotees call her base a home. She does not want people to gather around her and, as a result, set themselves apart from a regular life. Indian devotees like the word "ashram," however; they call her homes in both Germany and India ashrams. In a similar way they feel comfortable with the term "Divine Mother." Meera is Mother Meera, and Adilakshmi is Mother Adilakshmi.

A house's flat rooftop gives the finest view over the land that is to be purchased. The land is brown, dry, and untended. Some form of irrigation will have to be brought in for it to have much value. Boys run out past the thornbushes to form a human fence about the perimeter of the twelve acres. In the center is a hillock, again untended but with some small structures on it. It is the Muslim graveyard, but there are no Muslims left in town to tend it.

Bordering this land is the scene of Mother Meera's last visit to the village, when she was sixteen. The school building is single-story, with two rooms. This is where she sat on a chair in the dust of its playground, just in front of the verandah, so that all the villagers could come out to see her.

THE HOUSE OF HER BIRTH is no longer lived in, nor is it a shrine. A small white building, part of a row, it has a thatched roof and a sky blue door that opens directly onto the street.

High on the wall to the left of its interior, faint behind grime, are a number of photographs of Mother Meera gathered together in a big picture frame. Otherwise, the house is partly abandoned and partly a storeroom for abandoned things.

The main room, in which everyone lived and ate and slept, is about twelve feet wide and twelve feet deep. A wall that divides it in two is an addition since the family's time.

There are other changes too. A little cooking annex at the back was not previously there. The family cooked all their meals in the yard.

The yard is just a few feet wide, closed in by a high wall. Beyond this wall and above it is the tiled roof of another building. This is Venkat Reddy's home after his marriage, where the young Kamala spent some early years.

There used to be a window in this outside wall. The children of the family looked through it to spy on the comings and goings in the Reddy household on the other side. Now this window is bricked up.

The room where the goddesses were worshiped is full of rubbish, broken furniture and cases, and cobwebs. Among the debris are two treasures. One is a picture of the goddess Durga. The other is Venkat Reddy's death certificate, obscured behind dirty glass in a dark green frame. It will be cleaned and sent to Germany.

Young boys crowd the room. They are silent. One laughs, and then all join in. They find it funny that anyone should regard this modest little home as a very special place.

———◇———

THE MAIN STREET is made of red earth and is wide enough to act as a public square. A small rostrum is set up at one edge of it, space enough for a single person to stand and be raised a little above the crowd. Behind the rostrum is a tall red pole and on top of the pole the emblem of the Communist Party, a hammer and sickle fashioned out of metal. There are a couple of grocery stores here too, one of which acts as a café. A group of men pass time outside in its shade. It is the main thoroughfare for a village that had thirteen hundred people on its last electoral register, setting the present population at about two thousand in all. Electricity was introduced in 1969, and it is only the lack of more piped water that stops the village from growing much larger. Poorer houses, tiny, with roofs of thatch, fringe the outskirts of the town. These are the homes of the "untouchables." Though poor, Mother Meera's family is of the kshatriya caste and so had a defined place in the running of the village. These outcasts are left to live just out of sight of everybody else.

The working day takes many villagers up a path toward the edge of what used to be a forest, though it has largely been cleared. It is a country path, bordered by bushes and trees, with crops in the fields to either side. Mother Meera once considered buying this land too, but decided she wanted something nearer to the center of the village.

A journey of about two kilometers ends at the farm buildings in which Venkat Reddy and the young Mother Meera first found quiet away from the village.

The edge of this farmyard is marked by a well. Its opening is square, about twenty feet across, and its brick cladding drops some fifty feet or more.

This well plays a part in the Mother Meera family story. Veera and Antamma had six children altogether. Mother Meera was the third and Raju the last, with two daughters in between them. The elder son died of an illness at the age of eighteen. The youngest daughter died in this well.

They found her body after three days and carried it off for an autopsy. The body was so bloated, no verdict as to the cause of death could be reached, whether accident, suicide, or murder. Death was simply death. She was eighteen years old. Her death marked the end of an unhappy marriage.

The family that remains is commanded by Mother Meera not to speak of the event outside of their own intimate circle. The deaths of her sister and older brother are personal tragedies that do not belong in Mother Meera's myth.

The place is still worked as a farm. Cows and geese are gathered between the tumbling walls. A new giant well has been dug, but no brick facing added to it yet. A small mango orchard has been planted, young trees with healthy dark green leaves that drop small patches of shade onto the ground. Just beyond the farm buildings are a few individual tombstones. A yellow one memorializes Venkat's mother-in-law.

The estate is reduced to forty acres now, down from two hundred. Mother Meera was once prepared to buy the remaining forty acres from Mrs. Reddy, Venkat's wife. "Business is business," Mrs. Reddy replied to Jyoti's objections to the sale. She had negotiated a high price, so she would sell. The deal foundered on one point. Mother Meera insisted that Mrs. Reddy make the journey down to visit her in Madanapalle first. Mrs. Reddy refused to go, holding to the more normal custom that if any meeting between the two parties is necessary at all, it is the purchaser of land who travels to close the deal.

—◇—

THERE ARE TWO TEMPLES in the village. Both are supremely modest. One is the Poshamma temple. Happy to simplify matters, villagers call Poshamma "the village goddess." Her temple is a miniature one, about five feet square. Its ceiling is so low only a child can walk upright inside. There are two rooms. The goddess Poshamma is represented by an outline carved into a small block of black stone in the rear chamber.

The roof is stacked with shards of broken pottery in place of proper tiles. The walls are large blocks of stone. They are ancient and weathered. The elders will ask Mother Meera for funds to repair the temple. There is no obvious show in the village of reverence for Mother Meera as a divine being, but she commands considerable respect for her wealth.

The other temple is on the fringe of the village, near its reservoir. It is smaller than Poshamma's, though higher. Like a cage, a wrought-iron gate forms its front wall. Inside is an image that bulges out of a rock. It is painted a bright red to look like some exposed internal organ of the earth. It is possible to see the form of Ganesh in the rock and make out his curling trunk, but in fact this image represents the monkey god, Hanuman.

—◇—

A SIDE LANE leads from the main square to a grander house, with only walls for direct neighbors. This is the house of Mrs. Reddy, Venkat's widow.

Born with a spot on her tongue, which local folklore holds gives her the ability to have her curses come true, she has used the power only once. "May his body rot and be eaten by worms," she wished for her husband.

In the West this may not be so surprising an end for a human body, as we are accustomed to laying our dead in graves. In India cremation is more customary, and burials would be in tombs and not in the ground. Venkat duly made the journey to the West, and Mrs. Reddy saw that his body was already rotting with disease. After his death he was laid in the soil of a German grave.

The end of a marriage is seldom easy. When Mrs. Reddy was about to get married, her mother told her she was making a great mistake. "It's the greatest truth of my life," she now says. Before Venkat died, though, she felt a great sense of peace descend upon her and knew that matters between herself and her husband were resolved, calm, and good.

Years later she returned home and went to put something away in a wall cupboard. Normally she did so without thinking, a simple brisk action, but for some reason this time she opened it very cautiously. Sitting on a shelf inside, looking directly out at her, was India's most deadly and sacred snake, a cobra.

"And you know," she told her daughter later, "it had your father's eyes."

Mrs. Reddy wears a sari of bright, shiny light blue. She passes across her house, from one shadow to another, like the break of day. Her face is round, her hair thick and black and shiny with health, her body strong. Though she prefers to stand at a distance, with the shadow of a recess just behind her, there is no nervousness about her.

Pictures of Sweet Mother and Sri Aurobindo hang on the front beam, prominent from the entrance to the house. Mrs. Reddy moves to show more photographs of the couple on a wall of the room to the left. She tells how she went to Pondicherry in 1956 and stayed in the ashram for twenty years. She is excited to speak of Mannikyamma too, the holy woman who lives in silence on a hilltop. She is quite sure of her greatness.

And Mother Meera, the girl she knew as Kamala?

She smiles and shakes her head.

"I do not believe," she says.

AN ANCIENT FORTRESS traces its walls around the summit of a rock that rises from the Indian plains. The town of Borngiri grows within the rock's shadow. Veera Reddy, Mother Meera's father, looks as out of place here now as when he first stepped from his village to this, his local town. A policeman has led the Westerner who was with him away to be questioned. Veera sits on a bench in the bus depot, dressed in startling white, trying to pull his body back from the attention of the curious crowd that presses around him. The crowd has many, many questions. In response, he holds up the pewter locket that hangs around his neck. The locket carries a portrait of his daughter. He invokes her name and her divine status and backs it with a smile of his own. Mother Meera is his daughter, his explanation, his protection.

The policeman returns the white man and raises his stick to drive the crowd away.

LINGA REDDY holds his new books under his arm. One of them contains paintings by Mother Meera showing Venkat's journey after death.

Linga remembers Venkat as his older brother. And as his best friend. When they were young, wherever Venkat went, whatever he did, he allowed Linga to go with him.

Linga is sixty-seven now. Venkat left home to get married and passed his portion of the family acres to his three brothers. Only Linga remains, in a house directly behind the one where he was born. Portraits of Hindu gods are tacked to the main beam of his front room, a photograph of Nehru, India's first prime minister, prominent between them.

Correspondence from Germany arrived in the house shortly before Venkat died, but it only dealt with business matters. Linga goes to the drawer where he will store the new books sent to him from Germany, books that include the paintings Mother Meera made of the journey of his brother's soul after death. He returns with two photographs. One is the picture of Sweet Mother his brother gave him. The other is a fading color snapshot of Venkat surrounded by flowers in an open coffin.

He blushes, but also smiles as he looks down to the floor, remembering lustier times. How did his home village react when Venkat reordered his life to be with the young Kamala?

"There was much talk," he chuckles. "From everybody. So much talk."

——◇——

NARAM REDDY lives in an ashram in Andhra Pradesh run in the name of Aurobindo. His body is folded into its basket chair, as though it were washed and starched within the white linen of his clothes and set to dry in this position. He speaks when he chooses, and otherwise not at all.

Other members of the ashram are around, and other visitors. They drink glasses of water and the conversation flows, much of it in Telugu. Veera Reddy is trading local gossip.

Naram continues to stare through his black spectacles at some space in front of himself. The words of the conversation are like so many mosquitoes. He copes with the buzz and only bats the questions away when they threaten to bite.

Venkat Reddy was his dearest friend, he says. They were the same age and shared the same interests. Though Venkat was married and he was not, they set off from the village of Chandepalle together and into the world beyond. They were concerned with social work and set up an ashram together. Then one day Venkat walked away and left Naram to run everything on his own.

That is enough. He will say no more.

"For more, you must speak to Jyoti," he decides. His finger turns the pages of his address book, one by one, and he leans forward to read out the Hyderabad telephone number.

"She can tell you what you need to know."

—◇—

"I ASKED MY FATHER why Naram did not help," Mother Meera's brother, Raju, reports. "Why he would not answer questions. My father says he was always like that. Even in the old days, when he was young and in the village, everybody preferred his brother."

The day has been mixed for Raju. He is unhappy in the Muslim quarter of Hyderabad, hurrying through its streets and bazaar, wanting to be elsewhere. Bookstores for the judiciary are to be found here. Adilakshmi is in charge of Mother Meera's gathering property and funds. She wishes to have a book on Indian probate laws, so that she can master the legal complexities of Mother Meera's will.

With the book under his arm, Raju goes to his favorite place in the city, the zoo. He laughs as an elephant sucks water from a pail, then bends its trunk around to give itself a high-pressure hose-down. Raju last came here as a child, with Adilakshmi and her brother Babu. Though he likes Adilakshmi now, he was not sure of her then, but adored Babu. He is still sad at the brother's death. Babu tried to live in Germany with his sister, but immigration became difficult. A proposed marriage to a German woman that might have solved this problem fell through. He returned to Madanapalle to run the Indian household of Mother Meera. One day, he and his brother closed themselves into a room and had an argument. When the door was opened, all that was found were the charred remains of both men's bodies.

Raju returned to India from Germany to take Babu's place in running the household. He is now twenty-one. If Mother Meera were male, she would look like him—long lashes blinking over large brown eyes as seemingly innocent as a child's.

Raju's mother and father share his home with him—yet he seems like an orphan, a young man made head of a household before he has left his youth behind, coping with responsibility he does not yet understand in a world that still puzzles him. He read in an early edition of *The Mother* how Mother Meera does not especially care for her human family and puzzles over this too. He does not know why the book contradicts his own experience.

He wants, very much, to complete his day out in Hyderabad by going to visit Venkat's daughter, Jyoti. Yet he knows this is expressly forbidden to him by Mother Meera. Instead he accompanies his father back to their home.

———◇———

THE POWER IS OUT in Hyderabad, so Jyoti sips lemonade on the roof of her home. Daylight catches on the turquoise of her sari and so shines more brightly.

"My father means nothing to me," she says, yet speaks about him for five hours.

Neon tubes flicker and buzz into life as dusk smears the sky, and Jyoti climbs down to the sofa in her front room. Her conversation continues.

"He still comes to me in my dreams. And I shout at him. I shout at him and I tell him what it is I really think."

There is always this, always the love and always the hurt. To contain both, she divides the memory of her father in two.

"One half thought of godmen all the time and was very intuitive, very sensitive to the feelings and inner lives of others. The other half was composed of a vast ego and sense of ambition. He couldn't take criticism and liked to be worshiped. After my marriage in 1975, I did not see a good quality in him. Before that there were plenty."

She tries for the good side once again.

"He was very intuitive, very empathic . . ." She falters a moment, then resumes with more strength. "But he was blind to others where his personal interests were concerned. He accepted people when they fitted what he wanted.

"There is one thing I shall always be grateful to my father for," Jyoti remembers, and smiles. "He introduced my mother and me to the Aurobindo ashram."

The resemblance between mother and daughter is close, and their ages do not seem that far apart. The daughter's hair is thinner, because she worries more.

She looks at the portrait of Sweet Mother that hangs on the facing wall. When mother and daughter speak of Sweet Mother, their cheeks flush in the warmth of smile. Then the memory of hurt drains Jyoti's cheeks, and the smile is gone.

"For my mother, at nineteen with a daughter aged three, her marriage was already over. It was not until she was twenty-six that she realized what she had missed in family life, and I know that she has not been sexually attracted toward other men.

"The village postman was my mother's classmate. He used to tell her all the secrets he learned about my father. My mother was more upset that my father was using all her money than she was by his unfaithfulness.

"My father knew people very well. He knew their weaknesses. My mother was strong, she could stand up to him, but in many ways she is also like a child. She loves to tell me stories of giants and dragons and gods, even though I am grown up. Her eyes shine and it's as though she is a child still and believing in all of this.

"I don't think of her as my mother. Aurobindo and Sweet Mother are my parents. They are my real father and mother. My mother is like a sister to me. I cannot believe my father was so cruel to her.

"He told his son-in-law, my husband, that my mother was sleeping with the postman. He told everyone this lie. My mother was not normally touched by such things and never cried, but she was very upset by this. My father knew everybody's weakest point. He knew just where to stab."

She sips her lemonade until air bubbles at the bottom of the straw, then sets the glass down.

"When my father had things in plenty he shared generously," she recalls. "If you say he did not care for money, in one way it is true. If he had money, he spent it. When others had plenty, he used that generously too.

"Also if you say he did not care for money, you must wonder why he liked the company of rich people so much. And why did he always say 'I don't care for money'? If something like that is true, there is no need to say it so much.

"When my husband began to earn good money, my father went around to the villagers and made them come and ask us to give more money to him.

"He often borrowed money. Kamala—I am sorry, I must call her Kamala, I can't call her Mother Meera—Kamala and Adilakshmi never asked where it came from, though my mother and I had to, because ultimately we were responsible for the debts."

She speaks of their last times together.

"I did not see him often. He came to my house here in Hyderabad every month or so, asking for money. At the peak of his demands he came every week.

"I always gave him something, even when times were hard. He was my father. What else could I do? Even though it was not my own money but my husband's, for I was not earning at the time.

"He followed me to my money box. If I took out, say, a hundred rupees, he would look over my shoulder, see that there was more there, and demand a hundred and fifty.

"Once he lost all the money I had given him. He came straight back and demanded more. He said it was my fault that the money was lost, because I had not given it to him with a clean mind.

"One thing I am grateful to Kamala for. She took my father out of the country. She took him away from us. If he had stayed, he would have been a terrible burden. We would have had to pay all his medical fees. He was expensive in all ways, not just financially. He was exhausting and demanding. He sucked out all my energy and my peace of mind.

"On all of his visits he never brought anything for my children. 'A beggar can only beg,' I said. I told Naram about it and he spoke with my father. Afterward, my father brought some biscuits when he came.

"I don't blame Kamala for all that's happened. I blame my father. She could not resist him. But I cannot look into her eyes. When I see photographs of her, see those eyes, my body shivers and I have to look away." She shivers now, with just the memory of it. "I'm sorry. But for me there is something malign there. Something evil in those eyes.

"You must be very careful. Very careful where you put your belief. Sweet Mother told a story of a visit she made to a French church. She watched an unhappy, depressed woman go in to worship at a white statue of Christ, but instead of Christ, Mother saw a spider sucking the woman's energy. The woman left in an even worse state than when she had come in.

"There was a cashier in the ashram in the time of Aurobindo. A great devotee, he wanted to sell all his property and give it to the ashram, but Aurobindo said no, you have a son, you must keep half. During the rest of his life he collected and wore many strings and talismans on his arm, sacred threads he had gathered from pilgrimages to spiritual people all over the country. At the end though, before his death, he had them removed, so that he could be only with Sweet Mother. My mother and I, we hope my father realized this truth at the end."

Outside her house she pauses to finger a plaque fixed to the wall. It reads "White Roses," for her home is named after Sweet Mother's favorite flower.

PART 3

A Journey into Life

CHAPTER 15

Coming to Grips

"Oh, so the Divine Mother is in Germany," the Maharishi Mahesh Yogi, founder of the Transcendental Meditation movement, says on seeing her picture in 1985. "It is very good to know Her to be there."

"I know her," the Dalai Lama says at his home in Dharamsala. In silence, for a long time he stares at her face in a photograph. Before he receives this photograph they have never met. "I have met her. But I am not sure how much she knows about Buddhism."

"I know her," the Tibetan spiritual teacher Gelek Rinpoche says after Mother Meera's photo catches his eye, smiling out from its place on an altar.

"I know her and she knows me," Mother Meera is reported to have said of Mannikyamma, the holy woman on the Indian hillside whom Venkat Reddy once visited.

A Peruvian shaman keeps Mother Meera's photo beside him through weeks of shamanic ceremonies in a South American jungle.

I am told that Sai Baba of Puttaparthi sends people to see Mother Meera and that Mother Meera sends people to see him.

It seems spiritual leaders all recognize each other in some deep way. Devotees long for a similar reciprocal relationship. They want to become what they revere, and so they hope their chosen spiritual leader recognizes them as an equal.

In the winter of 1996–97 a group of forty people fly out from North America to spend time at Sai Baba's ashram in India. They are pleased with themselves and their progress as part of a meditation circle, know themselves to be self-realized beings, and are confident that Sai Baba will be astonished at the power of their collective glow.

On their first day Sai Baba, floating in his orange robe beneath his halo of black hair, drifts across to the men's side of the gathering and speaks with a member from this group. The man tells Sai Baba how they are all teachers of the divine.

"No," Sai Baba smiles and waves his hand. "No teach divine. Divine, no teach."

The following day, he remembers them. As he draws near, he smiles and speaks.

"No teach divine."

They stay for two weeks. During those two weeks every group is given what every group longs for, a private interview with Sai Baba. Every group but one. The teachers of the divine have to make do with Sai Baba's public appearances and whatever they can glean from being in his ashram.

—◇—

IT IS POSSIBLE TO BELIEVE or disbelieve in Mother Meera. Her work continues regardless. It is also possible to disbelieve in the existence of oceans. This does not stop them from lapping the shores or swallowing fishing boats in a fit of fury.

Adilakshmi first saw the sea when she was twelve. The Bay of Bengal powered its waters over the temples it stole from the land and thundered across sands toward the carved rocks of Mahabalipuram. This town has been the home of sacred sculptors for many eons. This is where Adilakshmi heard divine voices for the first time, singing above the waves.

Faith in the supreme divinity of Mother Meera is complete for Adilakshmi. She sees it everywhere, even in those who are not yet conscious of it themselves. Faith in God is never absent, only latent.

German neighbors in their gabled house remain frosty toward the spiritual enterprise next door, but Adilakshmi only knows that the village of Thalheim is happy to have the supreme Divine Mother among them. She gives several instances of proof.

When the work on the house was complete and Mother Meera was not seen outside in the courtyard anymore, people were saddened by her absence from sight. When she traveled to India, the first burglaries in a long while happened in the village, and villagers attributed this to her not being there to guard them. The mayor brought his liver complaint to Mother Meera and was cured. The priest of the parish church attended an evening gathering and pronounced that it was good for his flock to also gather there.

Mother Meera surely appreciates the harmonious life that the village affords. Care is taken not to disrupt it. Visitors now make reservations in advance. They gather in a car park at the edge of the village and are led from there in small groups to Mother Meera's home. At the end of each gathering, they are encouraged to disappear silently into the night.

This offers sport to the villagers. How many devotees can they spot?

"Twelve!" a young man shouts to his friends on the dark hillside paths. "I've seen twelve *Mutter Meera Jungen!*"

—◇—

DANIEL, FROM HIS ROOM and music studio immediately below Mother Meera's own apartment, is amused at what those who come and go think of those who have a chance to stay in Mother Meera's home. He suspects they envy the time in between gatherings.

"But it is boring," he says.

There is no regular access to Mother Meera. People in the house find employment in the towns thereabouts, and their lives are geared toward the public evenings when they will get to see her again. The slightest news of any glimpses in between times gives them a sweet excitement. They enthuse over details of Mother Meera's dress and wonder at her purchases in the German supermarket, in just the same way they marveled in India at her purchase from an Indian merchant of many fabulous saris to be packed and shipped to her European base.

Daniel has switched his own creative interests from painting to music and feels the power of Mother Meera's support seeping down through the ceiling from her living quarters to his own. It suffuses his work and his home recording studio. When she is away from the house, he feels the power of her presence ebb away. And when Mother Meera finally goes away, as all in life must do, Daniel is amused to think of his room becoming a part of a museum and shrine in her memory.

There are few rules to living in Mother Meera's two homes. One is a ban on smoking. Men step out onto balconies to blow their cigarette smoke into the open air. Another rule is that no guests are allowed indoors without Mother Meera's permission. This makes for a very quiet social life for those who live there.

A stream fringes the back garden, and fields rise up the hillside beyond. Two white horses pull a farmer on his cart down from the village of Dorndorf. He attaches the horses to a plow and walks beside them as they stripe the land with newly turned soil. It is an archaic act of quietness and harmony that lends peace to the whole scene.

Mother Meera does not ask people like this farmer to believe in her. He does his work, she does her own. That is how the world progresses. She tells *New Age Journal:*

> If they want to feel, they can feel. I cannot force anybody to believe in me. . . . But it is my duty just to do what I do, whether they believe it or not.

Adilakshmi writes to me, "The Mother asks me to inform you that She never expects anything from you, nor from anybody. People are coming, having *darshans*, and going away." *Darshan* is her term for the process of coming before the silent gaze of Mother Meera.

We are to understand that Mother Meera expects nothing. Expectations are for people locked in the temporal condition, people looking for something that they do not yet have. Though they are an integral part of what is, has been, and will be, people have placed themselves in a situation of feeling apart from all that is.

In the magazine *Common Boundary* Mother Meera asserts:

> Although there is a human form, I have never been born as a human being. Divine consciousness was always complete in me.

This suggests that lack of divine consciousness is part of her definition of a human being. Every aspect of creation is divine, and there is nothing that is apart from God, but people replace this knowledge with the illusory and more constant sense of their own separateness. Humans differ from other forms of creation on account of their consciousness and use this consciousness to bestow on themselves a unique sense of separation. Mother Meera shares little of this human condition.

In that way, the fact that she has never been born as a human being is commendable. In another, it shows a sorry lack of effort.

Many people, very many among those who claim to lead a "spiritual" life, persist in a great reluctance to being born at all. They are sure that their true home is not here on earth, not part of a human family, but located on some spiritual plane they visit without their physical body. They never dare to realize the full glory, the full responsibility, the full joy that is the promised gift of being born into a body.

Denial of oneself as a human being is one of the saddest forms of separation a person can know.

—◇—

CHILDREN, LIKE ANIMALS, are usually more open to the divine. Adolescence and adulthood blunt perceptions. Adilakshmi is excited and happy one morning, a not untypical morning. She has just received a phone call for Mother Meera from devotees in Sweden announcing the birth of a new baby. The announcement comes ten months after the couple brought their request to Mother Meera for help in conceiving. They had tried for many years, and parenthood began to seem impossible.

Mother Meera seems especially willing and able to help with such requests. She likes to speak of the values of family life. Though children are discouraged from attending the public gatherings, parents are asked instead to pass on anything they feel they have received from Mother Meera's gaze by gazing into the eyes of their own children.

Why does the openness and receptivity of children begin to diminish at about the age of seven?

"When we grow up, the mind dominates and we are more involved in the world," Mother Meera answers. "When the mental, vital, and physical are dominating, we are not conscious."

So how can we try and keep our children in a fully open and receptive state for as long as possible?

"Be careful how we behave in front of the children. Behavior must be completely different in front of the children—keep out sexuality, dangers, emotional outbursts, don't quarrel and fight. If we can't control ourselves, how can they listen when we ask them to control themselves?"

When I show her the following parable, she accepts it as a reasonable comment on her work:

> Mother is in a classroom full of children, and she is the teacher.
>
> Some stand up and say, "You say nothing. I want my teacher to talk," and leave. Mother smiles at them as they go and continues to sit.
>
> Others feel anger inside themselves and storm out.
>
> Others want people to listen to their own ideas and go off to find an audience.
>
> Little by little the children disappear, and Mother smiles her blessing. They can come back when they are ready.
>
> A few remain, and Mother teaches on in silence.
>
> One or two children sit outside the classroom. They are so full of communion with God that they never think to come in, and Mother is happy for them.

——◇——

THERE IS ONLY ONE GOD, whom Mother Meera terms Paramatman. This God has many aspects and faces, but is still only one God. Whatever people worship, whatever name they give to their deity, their worship is of God.

Mother Meera explains to *Common Boundary* why the sense of separateness from God can be helpful:

> If we think that God is above us, then when we do something wrong, God can forgive us. If we think that we are God and we do something wrong, there's no one to forgive us. When you have full knowledge, you will know that there is no separation between humans and God, but until that time, it is better to maintain a dualistic attitude.

It has become quite common for people to look for "the God within." Mother Meera encourages us to externalize that search and look for God in her if we find we cannot go to God directly. It is perhaps a safer first step than looking for the God within.

"That's where there is great danger, where the ego grows vast," Adilakshmi states with confidence. "Of course all the scriptures teach us that the divine is within us, and this is so, but first we must accept duality. How can we go looking for the divine in ourselves? We don't even have the fundamental characteristics of humanity."

There is laughter.

"It is all right to laugh," Adilakshmi allows, a little bemused. "But it is right. When someone achieves some little thing, we are jealous."

=◇=

MANY WHO HAVE BEEN close devotees of Mother Meera subsequently claim their distance. There are different reasons. For some, the shift from being single to being married moves their focus to a different relationship. For others, the power of the charge they feel in her presence is too much. They are open, they are vulnerable, and the process is intense. There may be a psychological breakdown, perhaps hospitalization.

Mother Meera counsels that people should not take too much account of their visions and advocates the use of common sense. However, Westerners have to break from many of their received notions of common sense in order to follow Mother Meera at all. They prostrate themselves before a young Indian woman, attempt to surrender their lives to her, and then try to observe the effects of their actions in their lives. The bounds of their perceptions are widened, and so their hold on what they previously took to be the rational world is weakened. They take one step beyond their accustomed dimension, and their other steps are taken in space.

Mother Meera has termed such an arising condition as "madness," without perceiving any responsibility for it. In her professional role as someone who transmits a powerful force into those who come before her, there is a need to gauge the effects that such a surge of power will have. This sudden charge of power can be too much for some people, like passing a high-voltage current through a low-voltage appliance. They are left to go away and repair the damage caused. Their inner life, their visionary life, is in turmoil. Unable to withstand the pressure, they sometimes return to Mother Meera for another charge of power. As a cure for "madness," this has something of the subtlety of electric shock treatment.

Others part company with Mother Meera to follow a different spiritual path. When Jean-Marc, one of Mother Meera's earliest devotees, first met her, he felt she had a link with Christianity. He believes her assistance helped him toward a relationship with that aspect of God most essential for him. In the early days of the gatherings at Pondicherry, she asked him to find portraits of Jesus and Mary to hang on the walls. He stood beside her in a side chapel in a church in Trieste and experienced a tremendous power coming from the tabernacle. The force enveloped him and was typical of many experiences he felt when with her.

In Canada in 1980 he was extremely weak and unable to get out of bed. At the foot of his bed he saw Mother Meera with Jesus to her right and Mary to her left. He felt a great attraction toward Christ and the Virgin Mary and decided there was some choice to be made with regard to his devotion. He returned to the Roman Catholic church in 1986.

Others break away from Mother Meera for more violent reasons. Love flips to hatred. The writer Andrew Harvey was very close to Mother Meera, yet he now takes a public stance against her.

"People say Andrew is bad, but he is not bad. He is good," Mother Meera declares. "He is an angry child. When a child is angry, his anger must flow."

She states that time will see his return and keeps some distance from the public debate he attempts to begin. When others ask to write in her name to counter his attacks, she does not allow it.

I am a writer. My own love for Mother Meera also turned into anger and resentment. From the outside, devotion is often viewed as an anodyne experience. People see the shining eyes and switched-on smiles of devotees and are saddened. They see bright people brainwashed into simple-mindedness. They shut doors on the smiling faces, and old friends either remove themselves or wait for the crash of disillusionment.

The happiness of devotees is real and not spectral. It is the rush of young love that may even last a lifetime. Should the crash come, a subsequent stage need not be seen as a denial of all that has been. It can involve growing to the point where devotion to a spiritual leader is not seen as an aberration, but as a stage—an important, though not essential, stage in the process of awakening.

Mystical perception opens us up to a new world. When we are young in that world, we welcome the sense of a mother's all-embracing perception. And then we grow up.

Devotion is like a nest. We flap our wings and finally jump off into flight.

CHAPTER 16

Surrender

"You will have many doubts and questions," Adilakshmi predicts as I set off on my authorized quest to write my story of Mother Meera. "You must bring them all to us."

And what limits are to be set?

"You must write everything. Others' experiences, and your own experiences also. You are free, Martin. Completely free. You can go everywhere, see everything, and write about it."

I set off to India with my official list of people to contact who might help me. I contact all of them. Some are prepared to help, and others are reluctant. My research and stubbornness carry me further till I am meeting with characters from Mother Meera's biography who have set themselves in opposition to her. I do my best to diffuse their antagonism and hold on to my own perspective. By the time I leave India, I am quite ill.

I settle down in America to write my book. Mother Meera asks about my journey and where it has taken me. I answer. A fax arrives from Adilakshmi.

"Mother says not to write about India."

I explode. I do my best to return to stillness and write on. The subsequent work I intend to be a gift from my devotion. I submit it.

The reply comes. It informs me that my book is filled with untruth and must not be shown to anyone.

I visit Thalheim to discuss the matter.

—◇—

MY RECEPTION IS KIND.

"Mother is not angry with you." Adilakshmi tells me. "She lets you stay in her house, so you can see she is not angry with you."

This seems beside the point. I have no interest in her anger and cannot see that she has any right to anger whatsoever. On the other hand, I am proud and defensive of my own.

"Many, many thousands come to Mother. Mother lets you stay in her house, talk to people, go to India. There are many thousands, but now Mother knows who Martin is. You are in her heart. She loves you."

It strikes me that the name of Mother's love is being used as emotional blackmail to quell my spirit.

Mother Meera has been surprised at my speed. Six months after embarking for India on that overseas leg of my research, I submitted my manuscript.

"Andrew took many years writing his book," Adilakshmi says, referring to Andrew Harvey's *Hidden Journey*. "There were two thousand pages at first. It took a long time. Mother says that is the way. A good book will take three or four years.

"You should experience the joy in accepting Mother's 'No,'" she continues. "If we accept the 'No' and wait for Mother to say

'Yes,' all the responsibility for our life is the Mother's. This is a great relief. I have had to accept many such No's myself."

I suggest that they are withdrawing their support for my book because I have spoken to people who were not on their list of recommended contacts, most particularly to Mr. Reddy's daughter, Jyoti. Adilakshmi agrees that this is so.

I state how I have only written what I was told. People in India seemed to be telling me their truths. I know different people have different ideas of the truth, but surely everything I was told couldn't have been a lie. And usually I was able to cross-check a story and find two sources for it.

"We know Indians," Adilakshmi answers, from the depths of her own experience of being an Indian and a storyteller herself.

"You are a foreigner. They want to impress you. They will tell you anything. They will make up lots of stories. They are all lies. This book is not true. None of it is true. Mother is divine. The divine is beyond people's stories, beyond human comprehension."

I change tactics. I lament that the situation was not handled more artfully. I could have been strung along with the offer of editorial support at some inexplicit time in the future. Adilakshmi looks at me with compassion.

"This is not the divine way. Mother knows us like the palm of her own hand." Adilakshmi looks down at her own palm as she strokes a finger around it. "She knows where we hurt. Everything she does is for our own good."

———◇———

THE PREVIOUS WEEK, news bulletins all around the world were filled with film of Hindu statues, especially Ganesh. Devotees lined up to bow in the face of a miracle, as these statues were seen to drink milk that was laid in front of them. Mother Meera assures her devotees that the milk-drinking miracle is to be believed. It is the divine manifesting its power on earth, telling us it is here.

———◇———

AT THE CLOSE of this first editorial meeting with Adilakshmi I complain. I say I had hoped to be edited, not censored.

Adilakshmi greets me before the following evening's gathering, as I take off my shoes in the narrow hallway.

"I am an editor, not a censor," she assures me with a smile, and another meeting is arranged. My hopes rise.

The audience room begins to fill. Those who are here for the first time walk in first, a little unsure, a little dazed. Many have taken the walk downhill from Dorndorf, enjoying the softness of countryside. The village of Thalheim seemed gentle as it nestled below them in the valley, homes gathered around the spire of the church. Soon they were walking the village streets, and still there was nothing to threaten them. Any fears they had seemed to be fears inside, fears of doing the unexpected, of taking steps into the unknown.

Others arrived in cars, or in minibuses provided by local hotels, which do a thriving business thanks to these modern-day pilgrims, and everybody gathered in the village car park. People looked around them and saw people like themselves, quiet people in respectable dress. This gave them some reassurance. They stood beside the village stream and allowed themselves to be shepherded in batches across the village to Mother Meera's home.

Now they are inside. Adilakshmi is in strong form. An old woman shuffles in to the main room, white hair thick and loose below her knitted cap, her overcoat on, pupils glaring from the whites of her eyes, her face creased into a mask that will brook no disrespect from others. She wears her old age like a Bill of Rights.

"First row?" she asks Adilakshmi, heading for a seat at the very front.

"Second row," Adilakshmi says.

"They told me I could sit in the first row," the woman says, pointing back the way she has come.

"And I said second," says Adilakshmi.

A vast young woman sits down and blocks my view. Adilakshmi commands her to stand up and swap places with me. A strict choice is made regarding whom to favor at these public gatherings. Seats near the front are given to newcomers, to friends, to contributors, to the infirm.

When Mother Meera comes in, I have a clear view of her in her Victoria plum–colored sari. She looks very lovely and young. I am one of the first to move and kneel before her, my heart beating fast once again. It is good to look into her eyes. There is a gentle humor there.

Back in my seat there is a familiar switch inside my head, a call to greater attention. The body of Mother Meera glows in its white light once again, while some energy works to clean the wreckage of tired thoughts from my head.

Adilakshmi turns around as the evening moves on. She stares admonition and wags a finger at a lame woman who yawns. A few people now kneel in each aisle, signaling their intent to move toward the "waiting chair," the seat reserved for the next person to bow down before Mother Meera.

The evening draws to its close. It seems everyone has been up to her. Then a lone figure stands up and moves toward the chair, a devotee who has been waiting, patiently and hopefully, with the wish to be the last supplicant of the evening.

Then Mother Meera is left alone in her armchair, her head bowed, her body tiny. The silence continues till we are sure that there is no one left who wishes to come before her.

Mother Meera stands, and the movement stirs all who are in the room to stand as well. They turn their heads for a final glimpse as the figure of the young Indian woman pads her way out of the room and up the flights of stairs to her private apartment.

There is some movement now, some stirring of talk, some push toward the shop where Adilakshmi and Herbert will conduct brisk trade in books, photographs, and other souvenirs. In the audience room some stay seated in their chairs, collecting the experience of silence into themselves. A man opens his eyelids to roll his eyeballs out of sight and stare with the whites of his eyes, a public demonstration of bliss. Others wait to perform other acts of homage. They kneel before the empty chair and drop their foreheads to the ground in obeisance to the presence that still lingers there.

The cushion of the white sofa that held Mother Meera is wet with sweat, for Mother Meera generates a lot of heat during these sessions. This is the same bodily heat noted by her family during the illnesses of her infancy.

Such a heat has a place within the Indian understanding of the spiritual life. The term that is given to this is *tapas*. Yogis subject themselves to sustained periods of suffering in order to gain this form of psychic and physical energy. This bodily heat, or *tapas*, is kept in store, ready to be discharged like a lightning flash to melt whatever resistance it meets and in so doing act as a catalyst of change in the world. Indian scriptures tell how the gods make use of *tapas* too, most specifically for the purpose of creation. By incubating heat in themselves, they bring the whole universe into being. Their very perspiration is a form of their divinity left to mingle in the world and so transform it.

The sweat of Mother Meera soaks into the fabric of the cushion and then evaporates into the air as I walk out of the room and into the night.

—◇—

AT NOON ON THE FOLLOWING DAY Adilakshmi and I close ourselves into the book sales room for our second meeting. Adilakshmi carries a ring binder under her arm. It is filled with my gospel and decorated with a wad of little yellow paper squares. They are Post-it Notes, editorial comments on my book.

Adilakshmi lays her hands on the pages and looks up at me.

"Mother says you must erase this book from your computer and all your discs," she tells me. "And all copies must be thrown away. It must not be found in any archive."

As an opening gambit, it has immense authority.

=◇=

I WANT MY BOOK approved and the responsibility for it taken away from me. Mother Meera does not want it. I will come to admire the force of her will, perhaps one of the strongest wills in existence.

What must come to pass will come to pass. The rest is immaterial. She knows exactly and precisely what she wants from life and has infinite patience until it is drawn into existence. Nothing less than what must be will do for her. There is not an atom of room for compromise.

In terms of money and belongings, nothing is directly asked of anyone. If people wish to make gifts, they may do so. Many are made. It seems that considerable wealth accrues in this way. I know of cases in which gifts were quietly returned, because it was felt that the donors still had need of what they were giving. I know of cases in which Mother Meera has given unsolicited and uncredited financial help to those in need.

We can give everything to Mother Meera. Our fears. Our shame. Our thanks. Our achievements.

Our newly written books.

We might hope for something in return, but we cannot dictate what it will be.

Mother Meera has the single-minded focus of someone who is doing a jigsaw puzzle. We see how absorbed she is in her work, rush around collecting thousands and thousands of pieces to give to her, and are delighted with our offering.

She looks at them all, reaches into the pile, and picks out one piece. This is the only piece that fits her picture. The rest are thrown away. We can look on with anger, frustration, despair, or delight at how our gift has been received. In the meantime she carries on composing her picture.

⬥

I DEFEND MYSELF. I suggest my book is geared to the Western mind.

"We are very Western," Adilakshmi counters. "We have been here many years. We read many Western books. When there is something people do not like or understand, they say, 'It is Eastern.' But it is just that they don't like it. People are people."

I make a declaration. I state the lesson I am trying to learn.

"You ask us to surrender everything to the divine," I say, "but that's not our way. We can surrender everything to the divine, but not our responsibility for our own lives."

"People never surrender everything to the divine. They work on, keep to their jobs and families and self-interests. *Darshan* is free. It is Mother who gives everything."

"Then why do some devotees feel disappointed?"

"Because their desires are not met. They have desires, but Mother does not think it right to fulfill them. That is why people are disappointed."

"Their desire is often to escape from their lives into spirituality," I suggest. "This is what Mother won't allow. There is no escape. She always sends us back into our own lives. That's what I mean when I say we cannot surrender responsibility for our own lives. That's why I can't just surrender this book."

"This book is not your life," Adilakshmi says. "Write what you like. Mother does not mind. Mother does not stop you. But this book is about Mother's life. It is different."

If so, that's what the editing process is about. We can work on this together. They can tell me what is true. Surely?

"Mother says everything must be erased," Adilakshmi repeats.

I try again.

"I know Mother Meera is a gateway to the divine. Through her I have come to see God, but . . ."

I become silent. My "but" seems a little silly. Surely if I have been helped to see God, that is enough. It is fair to be asked to do something in return.

"What was your 'but'?" Adilakshmi asks.

I try to remember.

"But I don't know what a divine mother is," I say. "It means nothing to me, and I want to be able to tell it to a Western audience."

"It is easy," Adilakshmi assures me. "You ask something of the Divine Mother, and she gives it to you. Then you know who she is."

I asked permission of Mother Meera to write her life story, and she gave it to me. I sold my furniture, my car, my books, my record collection, and all my belongings to fund what seemed the most joyful mission my writing life could aspire to. And now I sit at an editing session with Adilakshmi and my book is pared to extinction. All the drama and effort of the year's work is distilled to a moment of surrender.

I agree to erase the book.

The copies are trashed. The computer buttons are pressed. The work is gone.

———◇———

IN THE KITCHEN of Mother Meera's house I speak with a visiting Scandinavian devotee. He spent fifteen years as a close follower of Sri Chimnoy, living with his community. After he met Mother Meera he was asked to leave, and his friends of that time all turned their backs on him when he met them around his home city.

He traveled with Mother Meera and a few of her followers to India, where he worked on the construction of her house in Madanapalle. Two days before he was due to leave India, Herbert was taking him indoors for a short break to work on the computer. Mother Meera stopped him and sent him back to work.

"That's not why I paid for his food," she said quietly, in German.

He was furious. After the experience of rejection by Sri Chimnoy, his heart was bleeding and he longed to be told he was loved. This never happened.

At first Mother Meera was shy around him. Shyness is part of her nature in public. "Mother is Indian," Adilakshmi explains when I ask about it. "Shyness is one of the jewels of an Indian woman."

She has begun to lose some of this initial shyness when he is with her, but has never given him the words of love he was looking for.

He is getting what he needs, he is almost sure. His own love is strong. He trusts that though her love is silent, it is infinite. He admires the extent to which Mother Meera is free of her devotees. Many masters become steered by the demands put upon them, but not Mother Meera.

I begin to look for new terms to describe Mother Meera's love, terms like ruthless and dispassionate. Whatever it is, her love is not sentimental.

———◇———

AS THE FIRST FEW ASSEMBLE in Mother Meera's home to await her appearance for that evening's public gathering, Adilakshmi is radiant and talkative. An Indian woman wants to know what Adilakshmi's secret is. How does she manage to spend so much time in intimacy with Mother Meera?

"Love," Adilakshmi answers. "The secret is love. I do what Mother says. Sometimes I get blame. Sometimes I get praise. I take both. Truth is always bitter. Sugar-coated truth is not truth. Truth is always bitter."

Adilakshmi is in her orange sari. Mother Meera is dressed in a simple purple, with some cotton decoration in an orange elephant motif. I work to keep a strong focus on her while she is there. As she shuffles out of the room at the close of the evening, she no longer seems young.

AT OUR LAST MEETING, Adilakshmi brings a message for me from Mother Meera. It is advice for me if I am to continue the work that has led to this book.

"You have to be deep within the divine experience."

WE ARE TOLD to ask for everything.

Within a year of first meeting Mother Meera, in what now seems a lifetime ago, there was little left to ask for. My life seemed close to the peak of perfection. My first novel was published to glowing reviews and national attention and was short-listed for Britain's premiere first-novel award. A hundred friends gathered to celebrate it. I moved into an affair with a young man whom I had longed to be with for some time and who wafted like a gift toward me. It seemed easy to move from a position of wise celibacy into love and to come around to some public acceptance of my being gay. My newly written novel was greeted in manuscript with unalloyed glee by my publisher and my agent. I had a fine home of my own, and life was good.

Aside from owning a dog, which was given to me for a two-week spell the following summer, this was the sum of all I wanted.

It lasted a couple of weeks.

The most powerful review of my book was due. *The Sunday Times* treated it to a full half page. The review was venomous and hate-filled. The prize went elsewhere. The paperback deal for the novel evaporated. Enthusiasm for the new novel switched to disregard. Some friends stayed, others vanished. The love affair was one of those brief, exuberant blossoms. The young man said good-bye and walked away from our friendship to sleep with others. Rot was discovered in my ceilings and walls. My home, quite literally, fell apart as rain flooded in through the roof.

Nothing lasts forever. Two weeks seems briefer than was necessary. I had more capacity for enjoyment in me than that, but then being with Mother Meera seems to accelerate every process.

I tucked my life into a corner of my kitchen while my home was rebuilt around me.

———◇———

MAGGIE, AN ACQUAINTANCE, stands at the upstairs balcony of her English cottage. She looks down and sees her own body crumpled and twisted on the floor in the hallway.

"This is what you will go through," an inner voice tells her. "Are you prepared to accept it?"

She decides she is and enters the final stage of her young life.

For all she knows, she is very well. She is a successful novelist, and her novels are awarded prizes and made into films, but she already knows the novel she is writing will be her last. She will write no more after this.

This experience is common, though in different degrees, with many who come to Mother Meera. They decide their old ways of working are no longer valid. The source of their work shifts from their minds to somewhere deeper. Work is the outer layer, it is the ripple from the fall of a stone in water, the slipstream from a journey, the expression of something that has already happened. When the quality of the original experience is altered, it takes a while to appreciate it. You are tied to the old patterns. You try to recreate the ripples without the stone. It takes time. The chatter of the old expression grows still as the new one arises.

Maggie is a devotee of Mother Meera. Her first contact comes from reading a book. She sees Mother Meera's picture and at the end of the book finds the telephone number of her house in Germany. She reaches for the phone, but as she does so she realizes that no phone is necessary. Since Mother Meera exists as a divine mother, she can contact her directly. Accompanying the realization is an immediate inner communication between the two. She feels she can talk with her, and be heard and responded to, as freely as if they were sharing a phone line.

Maggie's writing ebbs from her and she wonders what will replace it.

There is a pain in her head. An opportune sequence of doctors and ambulances sees her in a hospital bed. She has aplastic anemia. The pain is extreme and death pretty much inevitable. She accepts the whole process with an astonishing degree of calm, believing that Mother Meera is guiding her along the way. From her hospital bed she edits the galleys of her final book. All she asks is that her partner, who can find no personal association with Mother Meera, begin to sense her in his heart. As he sits with Maggie, the love between her and Mother Meera reaches out and floods him. His own work as a composer will now have to recollect itself and grow to accommodate this new awareness.

Maggie is very sick, quite peaceful, and will shortly die. She has tickets and reservations to go and see Mother Meera in Germany.

I go in her place.

———◇———

I AM SLEEPING in my bedroom at a German guest house, but in a dream I am in my apartment block in Glasgow. I rush across a wide, sunny road outside of it and into a dark, narrow close. There is a light switch on the wall, but when I try it there is no light. I rush back to my block, slam the glass door shut, and lock it with the keys that hang on the inside.

A young Indian woman comes to the door; she has close-cropped hair and is wearing blue jeans and a yellow body-hugging top. Her name is Gita. Behind her is a crowd of children. "Martin," they call. "Martin. Martin. Martin."

They are calling me onto their wide, sunny road. I have never known such terror as I feel throughout this experience. I try to give voice to Mother Meera's mantra to protect myself, but the words will not come. For a while, even my breath does not come. I gasp at the edge of death from fright.

I write something of the experience in a letter, my first letter to Mother Meera. I have a question. I need to know whether to leave my old life in Glasgow, sell my home, and be ready for something new. I pose this question in the letter, say I will phone her for an answer, and set off on the walk to deliver it.

It is dawn. Light touches the village streets and stirs an old dog into life. A car is coming down the street, but the dog does not care. It has a job to do. It stands in the middle of the road and stares at me. The car slows and swerves around it.

It is a small, squat bulldog, so old it has more gums than teeth. Its movement is steady, and almost appallingly slow. It stands absolutely still.

The animal world has no more complete expression of Englishness than the bulldog. The bulldog has that solid, immovable quality we English like about ourselves. Its stiff upper lip seems to curl around to form its entire face. England chose the bulldog as its mascot when hosting the 1966 World Cup Finals.

This bulldog on the street of Dorndorf represents me. This dear, sweet, ugly old thing is the embodiment of my culture, the way I am conditioned to live. Around the dog is an invisible sphere that fills the whole street so that there is no way around it; it is a tangible envelope of fear. I am very comfortable with dogs, but feel that this one will leap up with its arthritic legs and clamp its gums around my neck.

It has to be an irrational fear. I can see that. The fear has to have its source in me rather than in the dog, even though I sense the fear as being outside myself. The dog is feeble. The fear is a fear of myself. I can turn around or walk through it.

I walk through it, walk beyond it.

It is a silly thing, but it takes courage. The dog does not even turn its head. On the other side of the fear, the experiences of the night lift from me. I walk light-footed down the hill to drop my letter into Mother Meera's letter box.

———◇———

I TRY TO MAKE my promised phone call, but the line is always engaged.

As I walk down to the evening's audience with Mother Meera, a woman who is to become a good friend walks beside me. She is a Jungian analyst and helps me work through my dream. I see that I am clinging to my darkness like a baby to a security blanket and that I am in terror of the bright, open road that leads away from it. I see that the keys in my dream are on the inside of the door, and though I can be called to step outside, I have to unlock the door for myself. I have to dare to step away from my fear of freedom. The name Gita translates as "song," and the Gita, or song, of my dream is Mother Meera. My mantra dried within me when I tried to use it, because it was composed around Mother Meera's name and I was trying to use it against Mother Meera herself.

We invest others with the fear we have of ourselves.

My answer came without a phone call. I prepared my home for sale and got ready for the long open road.

———◇———

MOTHER MEERA DECLARES her way is a "way of joy." When we are in the throes of our own dramas, that joy often seems elusive. We are attached to pain we once suffered, we hold on to its ripples, and it hurts to let it go. Our old pains help define us, and we like the comfort of our definitions. We have sights fixed on our future too, a future we have already earned with countless small sacrifices. It hurts to be led toward an alternate future, one we have not earned through sacrifice. We want to play through. We want to beat the odds. We want to do it all our own way.

So we suffer away.

This is not Mother Meera's way. It is our way.

=◇=

MOTHER MEERA TELLS *Quest* magazine:

> Pleasure comes from outside ourselves, whereas joy is always
> found within. When people focus on the interests and needs of
> the mind, vital, and physical, joy is not felt very much, but by liv-
> ing in harmony with the soul, joy fills the mind, vital, and physi-
> cal. In following this path, you need not do formal worship. Just
> by doing sincerely what you do, you can find joy. If your aim is to
> find God through joy, you will find the way.

Divine humor is good for a laugh, often a retrospective laugh.
My bulldog was funny. A friend who was with me on that visit
wrote her own first letter to Mother Meera during this stay.

Writing that letter is an agonizing rather than a spontaneous
process for her. She is racked with headaches and stomachaches
throughout the week of its composition. She has to work through
the filters of difficult childhood experiences to manage the letter
at all, and the prospect of delivering it is a tremendous ordeal. She
has heard about my bulldog, fears dogs, and is terrified she will
meet the beast herself.

At dawn of the final morning she sets out on her delivery.

There is no dog. She reaches the footpath that passes down
through the fields. On the right, her head dipping into a sea of
rich grass as she grazes, is a young roe deer.

=◇=

"YOU ASK SOMETHING of the Divine Mother, and she gives it to
you. Then you know who she is."

Adilakshmi's advice cannot be as simple as it sounds. No
mother needs to prove herself by supplying gifts on demand. That
is just a recipe for a spoiled child. To test out the advice, and so a
divine mother, there are three steps to take.

First of all, we have to do some of the work for ourselves. We can't just ask for a new bike or a new car. We have to find what is an appropriate request to make of a divine mother. Then we have to summon enough faith and daring to make the request. Finally, we have to recognize something of the scale of the response.

———◇———

ON THAT FIRST AFTERNOON of my return to Germany, when I am seeking Mother Meera's approval for my manuscript, I am lying on a bed in her house. Words come to me. They make no particular sense, and so they repeat themselves.

"You have the gift of not being your father."

I write the words down, but they still make no particular sense. Nobody is their own father. I cannot see why such a fact is a special gift to me. I do not as yet relate it to my previous visit to Mother Meera.

———◇———

AT THAT TIME, eight months before, I am also lying on a bed in Mother Meera's home. It is nighttime and totally dark behind the shutters of my room. Even so, I know when I open my eyes I will see my father. He has been dead for over ten years, and despite that I know he is there in the room with me.

"I love you. I love you. I love you," I say, to prepare both him and myself. "I'm going to open my eyes now, and I will see you."

I open my eyes.

The room is dark. I cannot see my father, but he is there nevertheless. I reach out and touch him, hold his sides between the palms of my hands. He is thinner than he was when he lived, but though he has lost a lot of weight, he is still there in some very real substance.

I hug this being to me. We stay this way for some time, then this being that is my father merges into me. He passes through my skin to become a part of my body.

My father has always been a frequent visitor to me since his death. At first he came in dreams in which we gave each other guidance. Lately it has been in a more physical form. There is nothing I can see, but I have a very clear sense of his arrival and presence.

When I was a young teenager, we sat beside a swimming pool in Morocco and shared our only conversation about the afterlife. He said he felt that after his death he would live on through his children—not in the simple genetic sense, but that he would actually find some afterlife by inhabiting the bodies and lives of his children.

I go back to sleep, and when I wake the following morning I write to Mother Meera. Perhaps this relationship with my father is fine the way it is. It does not disturb me, but it puzzles me. I have one fear about it. Perhaps he really does not know where to go in death other than back to me. I ask Mother Meera to give him guidance if he needs it.

Adilakshmi carries my letter upstairs to Mother Meera and gives me her answer the same evening.

"Mother says she will help. She will help you." Adilakshmi smiles. For a while it seems that the answer is complete. Then she delivers Mother Meera's final words, almost as an afterthought. "And she will help your father."

I am surprised at the answer, surprised that the help is promised to me, first of all, when I was only asking for help for my father. But I am also pleased and relieved. I need not worry about the issue anymore.

⎯◇⎯

MY FATHER STOPS visiting my dreams. I presume all has been taken care of, and a few months later I embark on a miserable summer. I spend it with my family. My mother, stepfather, and sisters each live in relationships of their own, but my principal relationships have only been with each of them. Now that has changed. I am in an independent relationship of my own, and it is a gay one. They need time to accept me in that role.

It is hard for them. For some of my family the process is easier than for others, but there is considerable anger and considerable sorrow. For a couple of weeks I borrow a friend's apartment so that I can hide myself away and cannot find the strength to walk beyond the end of the street.

The process is a tough one. In accepting qualities in myself I used to think were unacceptable, I have to cast off other roles I have been playing. I am not the father to my sisters, but the brother. I am not the husband to my mother, but the son. Not the rival to my stepfather, but the friend. Since my parents' marriage fell apart, I have been working to heal the wound that it caused in the family, trying to replace the element in the family that has been lost. I am trying to be my father.

The summer closes. The family is mending.

———◇———

MY LAST VISIT to Mother Meera is just over. My book on her life is erased. I sit with James in an apartment overlooking New York's East River. The sun reflects off the steel gray of its waters. I tell the episodes of the summer and discover for the first time all the power in those silent words I heard while lying on the bed that first afternoon of my visit.

"You have the gift of not being your father."

The reasons for my loneliness, for my fear, for my anger, for my satisfaction I locate outside of myself. I externalize everything. I once thought it was simply a question of my father inhabiting me. Now I see how I have been invoking him all the time, calling him into existence all along, playing out the residue of his life in my own.

My question to Mother Meera set a process in play. I asked for help for my father and received the promise of help—help for myself and help for my father. I thought I was handing responsibility

for my father over to Mother Meera, but my request brought unknown responsibility with it. I made a request and thereby com-
mitted myself to its resolution. I had to work hard to release my
father so I could be true to myself.

The passage through life with Mother Meera takes work. It is
not a passive submission to divine grace. It is a readiness to com-
mit to all that life has to offer, to pry one's grasp away from all one
holds on to, to listen when one's life begs for the freedom to fulfill
itself.

As I sit in that New York apartment I am flooded with gratitude. I realize the extent of the response to my request. Adilakshmi was right. I now know what a divine mother is. I vow that I
will never forget this moment and this gratitude and come back to
it whenever my doubts arise in the future.

The vow and the gratitude I feel at that moment in New York
last for a few months, drifting in and out of my consciousness.
Then they stand aside completely to make room for a raging
anger that insists on having its say.

CHAPTER 17

The Quality of Light

Time passes. There is a shift of continents. A friend is inspired in the name of Mother Meera to rent James and me the refuge of a small house. It is in a village in the Pyrenees and its rear wall is simply the bare hillside, making the house as damp and musty as a cave. My story shifts from America to France.

This is an ancient village. The houses form one organism, composed of local stone. They follow the contours of the hillside, narrow walkways climbing between the curious angles of their walls.

The church tower crowns the village. Back in the thirteenth century this was the home of Cathars. The Cathar symbol still marks the fountain, spring water thumping with constant force down into the stone trough below. Because the Cathars did not survive to write the history books, they are known as heretics.

Their heresy was their belief that it is not necessary to pass faith in God through a religious institution. It is possible for humans to be in a direct and personal relationship with God.

For their belief the Cathars were slaughtered by the armies of the church.

A wild narcissus on a rockface is my first real taste of a Pyrenean spring. Its flowers are miniature and yellow, twin trumpets blown from stems of so light a green I can see the sap within them. I sit beside them.

Since erasing my book I have been stretching my devotion to breaking point. Every day has started before Mother Meera's picture, a journal open before me. I sit for an hour and see if any words will come, see if I can find my way into starting my book on her life from scratch once again. The devotion is forced. It is a mask that covers great anger.

A publishing deal for another book is close to being signed in New York. The publishing house is excited. The editor has visited Mother Meera herself. Mother Meera promised me help with my other writings, and I have been saying her mantra internally at each of my meetings.

Then the deal is snatched away, the publisher's interest evaporates. I have no money, and no apparent career. Anger fills every part of me. It seems I have trusted in Mother Meera, trusted in others, for too long. It is time to trust in myself.

"It's life or death," I say to James, who is fresh from his own visit to Mother Meera's house, where he received my long letters attacking him too. "I have no choice. I have to write the book. Mother Meera says something is untrue. I think it is true. I presume that divine truth is something different from my truth, and so I give up my hold on truth. Now I have to reclaim it. I have to write my truth."

The book starts again. It is fueled by anger. When the pace slackens, I search for my anger, retrieve it, and rev up again. In two weeks a full new draft of sixty thousand words is completed.

————◇————

OUTSIDE THE FRENCH HOUSE each spring day brings a delicate surprise. Flowers I have only known as tame garden specimens rise untended from the mountainsides. Irises fold back the dark and the light blue of their petals, striking poses next to each other high above the green. The light purple flowers of thyme spill down across the rocks of old vineyard walls. Rampant bushes of rosemary are dusted with their own floral blue. Soft leaves sprout to cover the naked limbs of fig trees.

Creatures awaken too. Small clouds of butterflies trail by, at home between falling cherry blossoms as they dance between the flowers. Salamanders, frogs, and snakes are whirled down the waters of the old irrigation channel and pause at a grating in front of our house. We rescue them in an old bowl and carry them down to the river's edge.

Bats sweep above the water at night. We watch them stream from the gables of the house behind our own, black silhouettes in the dusk that race just above our heads. In the daylight the bend in the river is patrolled by a heron and a light-brown falcon who owns the whole valley. We stand at the kitchen window and count the trout as they pass through the river's clear waters.

Many is the time James or I step to the window and look down into the waters of the river, to check for any splashes. We can see a soft and constant rain pouring down from the sky. When the rain is water that falls from clouds, we see the splashes. More frequently, though, it is a rain of light that makes no splash at all. It streams soft and white against the green backdrop of the hillsides.

Occasionally the light takes a different form, dancing and sparkling in a movement akin to snowflakes in a flurry of breeze. We never saw this light before moving deep into the experience we discovered through Mother Meera. Either the light is new, part of the light she is bringing to earth, or our perception of it is new.

I watch the light, I walk out through the hills. Slowly, the company of the landscape soothes me.

———◇———

It is the previous summer, at home in Santa Fe, and I sit down in a chair to meditate. It is not the chair I usually sit on. A large mirror faces it on the other side of the room.

A familiar pressure in my forehead announces a change in perception is about to occur. It is the feeling I have when looking into Mother Meera's photograph, before her picture changes and light bursts from its sides, the feeling I have before I see her body haloed in light as she sits in her silence at her public gatherings.

Now it is my own image in the mirror that changes. My face grows elastic and becomes other faces. A dim light gathers around the contours of my body, then flares into a light as bright and constant as I have ever seen around Mother Meera.

I look away, walk away.

When I return the light is still there.

And then, through the following days, I notice it in others. It seems like a barometer of their sincerity. When they speak from the heart or even sit still in some deep silence, they shine for a while.

This is before I come to France, before my visit to Thalheim during which I erase my book. When I am there, I tell Adilakshmi of the experiences.

"Mother says visions are not important," she tells me after listening kindly. I knew this would be her answer.

I still wonder what the light is. Is this Mother Meera's light now shining through me? Is it my light?

———◇———

And then I see that the light is no one's light. Light is light. An electric light bulb does not grow proud of the light that passes through it. The current is turned on, and it shines.

The current of life passes through the Pyrenees in spring. It passes through the Pyrenees in winter. It passes through me. It passes through all that lives, and everything lives. The cells that form my body are changing all the time. They flow in and they flow out. When my body dies, that flow will continue. Life flows.

Sri Aurobindo and Sweet Mother maintained that it is possible to find eternal life by working on a cell within the body to make it divine. Adilakshmi dismisses the notion. Even Sri Aurobindo's body was found to decompose, she says. It is possible to have the body disappear after death, but that is a yogic skill and is different. A body is composed of five elements like the earth, and until all the elements of earth change, a body will be what it is.

I come to see that humans have an infinite capacity, but it is not one of containment. The feeling that we can contain things handicaps our well-being. We try to contain our pain and our suffering. We try to contain our love. We try to hold on to the precious moments and never let them go. We contain an idea till it swells and swells and possibly becomes a doctrine. We contain aspirations, we contain our sense of all that life owes us, and sometimes we contain so very much that it seems bigger than we are ourselves. We pay homage to all we contain, although we fear its bulk as it masses around us and tremble sometimes at our relative insignificance.

We have an infinite capacity, but it is not one of containment. It is one of processing. Nothing is to be contained and everything is to be processed. Thoughts, feelings, experiences, possessions, they can be honored and appreciated and then returned to the flow.

Anger from my life burned through drafts of this book. Mother Meera's rejection of the first book I presented to her was the catalyst for this whole eruption of anger into my awareness. It burned and it burned and drove me forward, like the thrashing whip that spurs a donkey. Then I tired of running on anger and grew still enough to reflect upon it.

I had thought of myself as a docile person, one who didn't get angry. I came to see that something I thought of as depression, when every moment of my life seemed set against me, was nothing other than anger—anger I refused to admit to, anger I tried to contain rather than express, anger that was crippling me without my even knowing it was there.

I have as much anger as anyone. Mother Meera too shouts out her anger at times. Anger is not good, it is not bad. It is just anger, one of the forces of life. I don't want to work at its bidding, and I don't want to contain it. I want to recognize it for what it is, as soon as I can, and then release it.

═══◇═══

THE CURRENT FLOWS. I tried to pull myself out of its circuit and away from the current of life. We delude ourselves that this is possible and even right, but then we are absurd. Slowly, against my resistance, I was brought back into connection with what I call the divine but what is really the essence of living. Slowly, I was brought to see that what is so is so. There is one force that connects all life, that is all life.

It runs through Mother Meera as it runs through all of us. The difference is that Mother Meera puts up no resistance.

═══◇═══

IF I WANT TO LEARN TO COOK, I may trouble to go all the way to Paris and apprentice myself to a great chef. I may then become angry with the chef, because I also want to learn to drive and the chef cannot even handle a bicycle safely. I may walk away in disgust when I learn she is having an affair with someone who is not her husband.

If I do all of that, I am a fool.

If I see care and expertise and wonder in the chef's art of cooking, I should be satisfied with that. I can learn by that example. I should keep my focus on this aspect and not be troubled by the rest.

The same rationale applies when we visit someone we believe more spiritually adept than we are. The quality we admire in them is their being open to the divine. When they invite people to come and sit with them, they are doing a job.

Why do we go to them?

Our world runs on in its busy self-obsessed way and plays out its dramas. It is hard to know what other way there is unless we are given an example. This is the role of spiritual leaders. We come before them, open our eyes, and see divine consciousness at play. Nothing gets in the way. There is no separation, no judgment. For a glimmering of a moment we are whisked into a sense of divine play. We are seen for what we are.

Some say that the role of spiritual teachers is to reflect our own divinity back at ourselves. This may be so. It seems clear to me that the divine is alive within every human being.

What is the job of spiritual leaders? Their job is to display their quality of openness to the divine. That is the example we can learn from. If we rummage through other aspects of their lives, seeking more and more that we can copy, we are as foolish as the person wanting driving lessons from the chef.

———◇———

WHEN I FIRST VISITED Mother Meera and wondered "Is she for real?" I found some assurance in the mundanity of her life. If she is fabricating her role, it is one of the most boring existences in creation. Four nights a week, year in and year out, she invites hundreds of strangers into her home. She sits with them in silence for many hours, looking into their eyes and feeling their heads as each one comes before her. Then she retires from public view and lives quietly until the time comes around to go through the whole process again.

And again.

What is the future for Mother Meera?

Since her girlhood, Adilakshmi has had an intuition about an event that is yet to come to pass. She believes that the destiny of her life will lead her to water. Maybe she will meet this destiny in the building acquired by Mother Meera at the beginning of 1996.

In the nineteenth century a castle was built high above the town of Balduinstein on the River Lahn, a tributary of the Rhine. With its turrets, towers, and bulk it was designed to rival the creations of King Ludwig of Bavaria, the famed castles of Hohenschwangau and Neuschwanstein. For more intimate living space the family built themselves a magnificent chateau in the castle grounds.

The early 1990s saw an attempt to convert this chateau, Waldecker Hof, into a luxury golfing resort. With the work almost complete, the company behind the development went bankrupt. Mother Meera was alerted to the site as the real estate bargain of a lifetime, and the purchase was made. With ninety bedrooms, a large dining hall simple to convert into a public meeting room, and fine grounds, it provides grand scope for the basis of a large international organization.

Invitations went out to devotees, asking them to contribute whatever they could. Many took the opportunity to join the work-force. It was decided to replace the whole roof and raise the ceiling of the public meeting room by two feet. As the devotees labored, they were delighted to find Mother Meera working alongside them, her small frame once again summoning up feats of considerable skill, strength, and endurance.

Since Mother Meera has such a passion for real estate and construction work, it seems likely that more of these ashrams will be built around the world. She enjoys her privacy, so that it is unlikely she will gather many people to live around her. But because she already sanctions groups to gather and sit and meditate in her name around the world, communities are likely to establish themselves in her name. The next one will be based on the land she has bought for that purpose in Chandepalle, the village of her birth.

She states that she wants no religion to be set up in her name. This is perhaps a vain ambition. When Mother Meera has been absent from the room for just a moment, devotees fall down to worship the cushions she has left behind. She gives her official sanction to groups around the world who sit together in her name, with her image for company. It will take greater vigilance than Mother Meera shows to prevent a religion forming around her. Sweet Mother of Pondicherry, the primary role model for Mother Meera's way in the world, took exception to attempts within the ashram to turn her into an object of worship.

"It's *laziness* that makes one worship," Sweet Mother asserted. "What one has to do is become."

In preaching her own supreme divinity, even while asking that people stay with their chosen spiritual paths and allowing that there are other divine beings on earth besides herself, Mother Meera is requiring worship. Worship, after all, is the relationship humans offer to supreme divinity. The claim of supreme divinity does not leave room for much else.

The opportunity is there to tour the world, to attract media attention, to live as glamorous and splendid and adored and idle a life as she pleases. Mother Meera speaks of the possibility of world tours in the future, but so much prefers her home base to travel that trips tend to get postponed. Her weeks are patterned by her curious routine, the silent public gatherings and her German domestic round.

Mother Meera has chosen her life. It is a good example to follow as we try to choose our own. We can take from Mother Meera the chance to live our lives to the full. Once we have done that, there is no need to give our lives away in worship.

CHAPTER 18

Resolution

A spotlight trains itself above a screen on a nightclub stage in Santa Fe, and a sequined being called Musty Chiffon bursts into view.

Musty has all the bravura and gusto of a star. As a young boy, a future as a singing sensation budded within his nature. He let it flower, let it blossom, and absorbed into his being the personalities and teachings of two performers who had trod the boards before him. Mighty Mouse and Peggy Lee were the two exotic heroes in the myth of his early days. His voice broke, and his personality bloomed as a fabulous present for all humanity. Out of the body of a boy stepped the shimmering splendor of a drag queen who took her place upon the world's stage.

She slaps a tambourine against her fifty-year-old thigh and dances through some favorites from the 1960s. She dons spectacles and a silver wig and gives her heart to a Peggy Lee ballad. "Is that all there is?" she murmurs, and clasps her hands in an embrace of her own body as she glides across the stage. "If that's all there is, then let's keep dancing . . ."

She clothes herself in a vinyl dress of black and white Friesian spots and crawls through her audience, offering to be their cow. When she sings, it is with a fine, strong voice that stems from the inner truth she seeks to live. At the center of her act she pauses to share her wisdom with the audience, taking a sheaf of their written questions from the hand of her pianist.

This being Santa Fe, where spiritual quests are commonplace, somebody has posed a probing question.

"I want to worship the Divine Mother, but don't know where to find her. Can you help?"

Musty drops her eyelashes to seek her response from within, then opens her eyes to gaze out at her audience.

"Try looking in a mirror," she suggests.

She pauses a while to see if more wisdom might come forth, and it does.

"Have you looked behind the back of your eyelids lately?" she challenges.

And soon it is time to change into a crisply tailored pink outfit and emerge into her encore, her greatest and most passionate hit song, "I Want to Be Like Jackie Onassis."

———◇———

Do I WANT to be like Mother Meera?

For a time I suppose I did. I didn't like my own life and so I wanted hers. I aspired toward divinity. I was not good at being human, so I wanted people to think of me as being more than human.

That's changed. I don't want to be Mother Meera, because I have discovered an unexpected happiness in being myself. And I give some credit for that to Mother Meera. Life has been tough since meeting her, for it has been an alchemical process.

Adilakshmi writes in *The Mother* of a soothsayer who visited Mother Meera when she was the ten-year-old Kamala, back in her village in India.

> He told her that she would live far from her parents, that she would be worshiped and famous when young, and that she was a goddess with the gift of turning all things she touched to gold.

Whether or not they were ever actually spoken, I am happy to find truth within the soothsayer's words. The process that began through my contact with Mother Meera has helped turn my shame to acceptance, my self-hatred to love, my ignorance to the beginning of awareness. I came before her, opened to her, and something that happened during that very act triggered me into being.

Into being what?

Into being more happily human.

———◇———

SOME MAY FEEL DRAWN to Mother Meera or some other such being, but feel unsure about stepping into the unknown. Stepping into the unknown is a vital part of learning from any teaching. We cannot already know what we have to be taught. Teachers must bring us to something that is currently beyond our capacity or awareness. We have to find the courage to take that first step.

What might happen then? What is the power of transformation that might be triggered by such a being?

It is beyond words. That is why it is often transmitted in silence. It is the same learning, the same transmission, as passes in the deep gazing between a mother and her baby. Simply being in the silent presence of a mother triggers transformation in a life.

———◇———

IS MOTHER MEERA A TEACHER?

"You cannot study with Mother Meera," Adilakshmi informs a devotee who asks to do just that. "Mother does not teach. She gives *darshan*."

This is the truth of the matter. A divine mother is a mother and not a teacher. A mother helps her child to grow into independence and a fullness of life.

Much of my very personal journey with Mother Meera has had to do with the acceptance of my homosexuality. I have released shame, rejected denial, and learned to live with confidence. One of the essential lessons I have learned is that my homosexuality is a wholly natural part of my being. I can no more deny it than deny the growth of fruit on an apple tree. Apples will grow, whether I believe in them or not. People may try to deny the fact of my sexuality, but when I leave their cities and the terror of their opinions, when I walk in nature, I know that nature denies me nothing. Nature is nature and accepts the natural in me.

I do not expect my own mother to understand my sexuality from my perspective. My nature is not her own. Yet she finds herself able to surrender her own expectations for my life, and so feed me from her constant fund of love.

In the first edition of *Answers Part 2* (1997), the following question appears:

Which type of sexuality is good, heterosexuality or homosexuality?

Mother Meera replies:

Heterosexuality is the law of nature. Homosexuality is against the law of nature.

Some may find this statement unexceptional because they agree with it. I presume those same people would see the horror in stating that blacks are inferior to whites and backing up this claim with spurious scientific data. While society is often so regressive in its treatment of gays that such a statement can be heard without a shudder of disgust, disgust is the appropriate response. The statement comes from somebody who has advised a close devotee that she possesses 80 percent of the full powers of

God. When someone who makes such astonishing and constant claims to the authority of God allows her opinion to be published, she is asking that opinion to be accepted as dogma. This is the same dogmatic stance adopted by the extreme right wing in many countries as a call for the persecution of gays, the secret code that justifies their extermination.

It is not possible to excuse the remark as an expression of a traditional Indian cultural point of view, because both Mother Meera and Adilakshmi demand that they not be considered in the light of their cultural background. They insist that their years in the West have brought them a clear understanding of the ways of the West and that they have transcended the limitations of an Indian perspective. They must therefore accept full responsibility for the inflammatory opinions they publish.

I recognize that since I know with certainty that Mother Meera is wrong in her condemnation of homosexuality, I cannot accept her word on anything else. And in that fact, I find some relief. We can value her silence enormously, yet we should place no greater trust in her opinions than in the opinions of anyone else.

I include an alternate dialogue with Mother Meera to set against her homophobic statement above. When the charge of homophobia first broke against Mother Meera in 1994, my partner, James, called her with a question.

"Do you have any negative feelings whatsoever about homosexuals?" he asked.

"How could I be against anyone for anything?" Mother Meera replied. "You must go deep into your heart, see who you are, and act accordingly. Then what could there ever be to give up?"

⸺◈⸺

IT IS HARD FOR DEVOTEES to claim authority over their own lives when the object of their devotion preaches his or her own divine supremacy and asks the devotee for complete surrender. Yet it is essential.

We must give to God what belongs to God and to our spiritual figures what belongs to our spiritual figures. We need not confuse the two.

Every genius finds his or her own specialty, usually with the assistance of a coach or tutor. Jascha Heifetz played the violin, Mother Teresa nursed the dying, Esther Williams swam with elegance and precision, Muhammad Ali boxed. Mother Meera gives powerful spiritual transmission that helps people bud into the fullness of life. It is a particular genius, like all those other forms of genius. But genius in one area does not necessarily transfer into another. I admire each of the above as foremost in their field, but I would not necessarily go to any of them for advice about human relationships.

I have met a power that comes from Mother Meera, and it transformed my life. It did not come from her words but from within the silence of her public meetings. This young woman of grace and power and silence is the public face of Mother Meera. It is as well to set aside the words of her books and the voices of the organization that has grown around her and speaks in her name. It is wonderful to know her through her silence alone.

Venkat himself defined the quality of Mother Meera's genius. "She is a superb channel," he liked to tell devotees. This does not mean she channels God's opinions. The idea of God holding opinions is quaint and absurd. Mother Meera's opinions are simply her own. What she channels through her silent presence is a transfiguring force that opens the possibility for a direct perception of God.

Because she has spent little time working on being a human being since she met Venkat at the age of eleven, she is weak in her relationships with adults. This weakness is masked by a domineering stance when a challenge arises. When a discussion with devotees grew too heated, when it seemed that Mother Meera was about to lose the debate, she stilled them all to silence with the challenge, "Who brings down the light?"

In sublime contrast to this, she is in her element when dealing with babies and young children.

I went before Mother Meera at first as a baby in her world of spiritual forces, and she took my head in her hands. She gazed into my eyes as I gazed back into hers, just as any mother does with her baby. Through the quality of her gaze my growth in life was set in motion.

I have come to sense that Mother Meera hides behind notions of her own infallibility. This is a failing, and perhaps it is inevitable. It is hard to step beyond the carapace of one's own divinity when those around you worship you as divine. Perhaps divine mothers are required to sacrifice the joys of human life whenever they go public.

Maybe we cannot coax Mother Meera into a more playful sense of her own humanity, but happily the process works the other way round. She can spark the play of divinity in each of us humans.

When I first saw the light of the Holy Grail emblazoned on Mother Meera's face, I realized that the journey I was beginning with Mother Meera was not a journey into the material of her life. It was not an escape into the world of legend and fairy tale. The light that she brings to earth, the light that fills her and is there for each one of us, is not a light of instant salvation. It is a light that is there to be worked with, to be drawn deep within ourselves on our journey of inner transformation.

Mother Meera gazed into my eyes and transmitted the light of her love. In doing this she became the Divine Mother in my life. This is a fact that is fixed and eternal.

The look from her eyes triggers a process of deep transformation in the lives of those who open to it. Her ability lies in the totality with which she is able to remove the personality of Kamala Reddy from her professional existence as Mother Meera. She is a channel through which the force and light of the divine are given clear passage. Open to Mother Meera, and we open to the forces that lie beyond her.

We often use intermediaries to approach figures of power, until we know how to relate to them ourselves. Mother Meera exists as an open door through which we can see and meet God. When we worship her instead of the power that passes through her, to some extent we are closing that door. We are putting something between ourselves and the divine experience.

Mother Meera accepts the role of a spiritual mother in our lives. When we wonder what our relationship with her might be, we can find a parallel in our relationship to our parents.

There is a time when our parents are the supreme force within our lives. We are small and feel safe within the strength of their protection. We believe they can hold back all the forces of the world.

There follows a stage when we grow to challenge our parents, when we become angry and try to advance by discovering our parents' faults.

Then we pass beyond anger and into a time of acceptance and understanding. We see through to the personalities of our mothers and fathers, understand their shortcomings from the inside, and tremble at this glimpse of their insecurities. And yet we see their love for all that, a love so huge that nothing will ever turn it, a love so profound that it extinguishes all limitations.

———◇———

WHEN ASTRONAUTS FLEW to the moon, their hearts were caught in wonder as they looked back and saw the beauty of the earth.

The moon remains beautiful and mysterious. It still draws our oceans into the highs and lows of tides. It still washes silver light across our nights. Yet our astronauts no longer fly there. We watched television coverage of the lunar landscape, peered back through space at our own planet shining blue against the dark, and our need to walk on other planets was eased. Manned space flights continue but content themselves with orbiting planet earth, for now.

Devotees see Mother Meera shine like the moon. They watch silver, white, golden, and other lights flare from her. And they launch themselves into the mystery of her existence. This is not a journey of no return. Like our lunar astronauts, they have the chance to look back the way they have come. They see their own lives shining with a beauty they have never seen before. They notice how the qualities that attract them in Mother Meera also radiate from themselves.

We traveled to the moon to appreciate the glory of planet earth. In a similar way a journey toward Mother Meera can be a vital step toward retrieving the wonder in our own lives.

In July 1997 astronomers reported seeing light from a galaxy some thirteen billion light-years away. This light comes from a time when the universe was only 7 percent of its current size. It is the farthest our civilization has ever been able to look—the farthest in distance and the farthest back in time.

Our bodies are made from matter created in stellar explosions. We can stand on the crust of our planet and look up at the stars. The light that we see has been traveling since years before our existence, since years before all that we can conceive of as existence. As the starlight hits our eyes, as the light enters our bodies, we are joined to the farther reaches of the cosmos. The light enters us, but of course it does not stop at our perception. Our seeing starlight does not extinguish it. The light is available for all who can see it, and then hurtles on through time and space.

The instant of seeing is an instant of belonging. Our moment of attention brings billions of years of history into the present. The light from a star is a constant beam. Through our sight we join the moment the starlight came into being, and we speed on with it into the light's entire future.

We each contain the universe as we walk around Mother Earth. To know so much gives a ravishing perspective to our lives. When we know that infinity is compressed into our every moment, we sense something of the value of all that lives. Love becomes our inevitable condition. Our life becomes a flood of appreciation.

First we must open to the light. To the light that falls to earth, be it from God or stars. All forms of light are aspects of the same light, varying only in quality. Light shines from the sun, from eyes, from skin, from within the stem of a flower.

In order to see the light, we must stop being consumed by our areas of darkness. In order to be the light, we must dare to let it touch our reserves of shame and bitterness. When we look into the eyes of Mother Meera, the love of a divine mother looks back into our soul. The light of that look is a call to action. It is a call to emerge from the shadows of our lives and truly live. We are shown all of our life's possibilities.

This is the essence of Mother Meera. We come to see her, and we are presented with our possibilities. The rest is up to us. We can choose to live in shadow—or in light.